SAFE CITIES

GUIDELINES FOR PLANNING, DESIGN, AND MANAGEMENT

by **Gerda R. Wekerle**
and **Carolyn Whitzman**

Van Nostrand Reinhold
I(T)P **A Division of International Thomson Publishing Inc.**

New York • Albany • Bonn • Boston • Detroit • London • Madrid • Melbourne
Mexico City • Paris • San Francisco • Singapore • Tokyo • Toronto

Copyright © 1995 by Van Nostrand Reinhold
A division of International Thomson Publishing Inc.
I(T)P ™   The ITP logo is a trademark under license

Printed in the United States of America
For more information, contact:

Van Nostrand Reinhold
115 Fifth Avenue
New York, NY 10003

International Thomson Publishing GmbH
Königswinterer Strasse 418
53227 Bonn
Germany

International Thomson Publishing Europe
Berkshire House 168-173
High Holborn
London WCIV 7AA
England

International Thomson Publishing Asia
221 Henderson Road #05-10
Henderson Building
Singapore 0315

Thomas Nelson Australia
102 Dodds Street
South Melbourne, 3205
Victoria, Australia

International Thomson Publishing Japan
Hirakawacho Kyowa Building, 3F
2-2-1 Hirakawacho
Chiyoda-ku, 102 Tokyo
Japan

Nelson Canada
1120 Birchmount Road
Scarborough, Ontario
Canada M1K 5G4

International Thomson Editores
Campos Eliseos 385, Piso 7
Col. Polanco
11560 Mexico D.F. Mexico

1 2 3 4 5 6 7 8 9 10 EDWAA 01 00 99 98 97 96 95 94

The authors gratefully acknowledge permission to excerpt from Statistics Canada publication, *The Daily*, Catalogue 11-001E, November 18, 1993. Figure 1.1 was adapted from this publication. *Reproduced by authority of the Minister of Industry, 1994.* NOTE TO READERS: Readers wishing additional information on data provided through the cooperation of Statistics Canada may obtain copies of related publications by mail from Publication Sales, Statistics Canada, Ottawa, Ontario, K1A 0T6 or by calling (613) 951-7277 or toll-free 800-267-6677. Readers may also facsimile their order by dialing (613) 951-1584.

Library of Congress Cataloging-in-Publication Data
Wekerle, Gerda R.
    Safe cities : guidelines for planning, design, and management /
by Gerda R. Wekerle and Carolyn Whitzman.
        p. cm.
    Includes bibliographical references and index.
    ISBN 0-442-01269-1
    1. Crime prevention—Planning. 2. City planning. 3. Violence
against women. I. Whitzman, Carolyn. II. Title.
HV7431.W397 1994
364.4'9—dc20   94-15736
                                                     CIP

CONTENTS

PREFACE

This book is a product of our personal and professional histories. It has grown out of our research, community activities, and passions. Both of us are confirmed lovers of cities. We live in dense urban neighborhoods in the city of Toronto and our travels frequently take us to other cities. Our roots in the women's community in Toronto and in Montreal have led us, individually and collectively, to focus on violence against women and how this relates to the planning and design of cities.

We began to work together in the summer of 1990, developing training sessions for staff of the City of Toronto's Planning and Development Department on how to incorporate issues of urban safety in planning and design practice. The seven training sessions we held that summer were attended by the majority of the planning department staff. Initially, there was a lot of scepticism about the project. Why should planners concern themselves with violence against women or with urban safety? Interest grew over the course of the summer and the last sessions were heavily attended as planners found that the information and approaches could be applied to concrete projects. Planning staff urged us to create a set of easy-to-follow guidelines that they might consult in their daily work and use as a handy reference guide. They promised to work with us to develop a set of guidelines and followed through by reading several drafts, making detailed comments, and meeting with us to discuss changes and additions. This guide was subsequently published by the City of Toronto Planning and Development Department and inspired other cities, including North York, Ontario, and St. Paul, Minnesota to develop their own guides.

We found that the working guide on safer cities was widely used. Within the city of Toronto, the Departments of Public Works and Buildings and Inspection used the guide to develop new initiatives. A Toronto-based architectural firm used it to develop the site plan for a new suburban community that paid extra attention to urban safety and incorporated this as part of their marketing. A suburban city used the guide in developing new social housing projects. The City of Toronto's Parks and Recreation Department commissioned a more detailed guide on urban safety in parks. Architects, developers, police departments, and community groups in North American cities, and as far afield as Japan and New Zealand, used the guide to assist them in thinking through specific projects. Toronto City Council adopted the Guide for use in the city's ongoing development review process.

Our continuing work with the City of Toronto's Safe City Committee also brought us into contact with new issues and new developments in the field. Whitzman traveled to Britain and Australia to learn about Safe Cities initiatives in those countries and to share with them our approaches in Toronto. In her role as Facilitator of the City of Toronto's Safe

City Committee, she works closely with politicians, city bureaucrats, and community organizations to develop municipal strategies to prevent crime. The Safe City office has also become part of a worldwide network of municipal Safer Cities initiatives. A new interest in Community Crime Prevention approaches in both the United States and Canada resulted in a spate of conferences, reports, and workshops. Increases in street crime and personal violence in urban centers brought the issues of community crime prevention to public and media attention.

This book blends our knowledge of current research, practical projects, and success stories from cities in the United States, Canada, Britain, Europe, Australia, and New Zealand. Our standpoint is that cities are vital and exciting places, and that all citizens should have equal rights of access to the streets and to urban services. Much of the new work on Safer Cities has been grounded in urban initiatives that pay attention to violence against women, fear of crime, and community-based solutions. Our experience in Toronto has shown that when cities can tap and reinforce these community resources the city is both enriched and galvanized to take action to develop strategies to make cities safer for all its citizens.

ACKNOWLEDGMENTS

This book has grown out of a project of the Safe City Committee, City of Toronto. We appreciate the support and enthusiasm of the Committee and its Co-chair, Councillor Barbara Hall.

We would like to thank all the participants in the "Planning for a Safer City" workshops, held from April to July 1990, whose enthusiasm and ideas helped shape this project. Vicki Obedkoff and Mary-Louise Work, working for the Training and Development Section of Management Services, City of Toronto, helped organize the workshops. We received comments from many staff in the City of Toronto's Planning and Development Department and are grateful for the detailed feedback provided by Amy Falkner, Leo de Sorcy, Helen Logan, Laurel Rothman, Gail Johnson, Maureen Fair, Blair Martin, Greg Byrne, Brian Milne, Mal Williams, John Gladki, and Commissioner Robert Millward of the Planning and Development Department. We thank Edward Tipping and Fred Breeze of the City of Toronto's Buildings and Inspections Department, P. Balint of Public Works and the Environment, and Dan Egan, City of Toronto Bicycle Planner for their comments. Discussions with Susan Addario, Wendy Sarkissian, and Regula Modlich helped in the revision of several sections. Vincenzo Pietropaolo applied his considerable talents to photographing safer and less-safe Toronto places. Frank Stoks of Coopers and Lybrand in Wellington, New Zealand encouraged us to embark on this project and offered his advice and support. The Metro Action Committee on Public Violence Against Women and Children contributed to our knowledge and graciously allowed us to reprint the Safety Audit Guide. David Orsini shared his knowledge of security in parks. Mary Vogel, University of Minnesota, provided advice and encouragement. Pam Macdonald, Director of Parking and Security, York University, commented on the section on university campuses. Linda Fice, Kathy Dean, Anne Morin, and Al Leach of the Toronto Transit Commission were supportive of the project and provided photographs. Wendy Lochner, senior editor, Van Nostrand Reinhold, saw the potential of this project and demonstrated patience in seeing it through to completion. Karen Franck offered useful suggestions that helped focus the book in its initial stages. Gerda Wekerle was funded by a SSHRC grant No. 410-89-0619 for part of this work. The Faculty of Environmental Studies, York University provided ongoing support. Carina Hernandez, Faculty of Environmental Studies, York University, completed the extensive word processing involved in the many versions of this book with a high level of professionalism.

Gerda Wekerle would like particularly to acknowledge the support and ongoing encouragement of Slade Lander and Bryn Lander. They put up with visiting hot spots of crime and photographing places that were not on the typical tourist itinerary with good humor and patience. Margaret Lander provided a New York base for completing the project.

Carolyn Whitzman would like to acknowledge the inspiration of working with a coterie of brilliant women making Toronto safer, among them: Susan Addario, Barbara Cowan, Ali Grant, Dawn Greenwood, Connie Guberman, Barbara Hall, the late Lois Heitner, Deborah Hierlihy, Sue Kaiser, Pat Marshall, Reggie Modlich, Jennifer Morris, Ann-Marie Nasr, Jennifer Ramsay, Shirley Roll, Lisa Rouleau, Sara Singh, Paddy Stamp, and Kate Sutherland. She would also like to thank David Hunt and Simon Whitzman Hunt for keeping her sane.

ABOUT THE AUTHORS

Gerda Wekerle is a Professor in the Faculty of Environmental Studies, York University. She has published widely on urban open space, housing, and transportation. She is co-editor of *New Space for Women* (Westview Press) and *Remaking the Welfare State* (University of Toronto Press.) She was a member of the Taskforce on Public Violence Against Women and Children of Metropolitan Toronto. **Carolyn Whitzman** has worked for Women Plan Toronto, a women's community organization in Toronto that pioneered participatory action research on women's planning needs in the urban environment and women and urban safety. A planner with the City of Toronto's Planning and Development Department, Whitzman became the first full-time staff person of the City of Toronto's newly established Safe City Committee in 1989. Wekerle has been a citizen appointee on the Safe City Committee. Both are members of the Women's Security Advisory Committee of the Toronto Transit Commission.

1

Introduction

Violent crime is *the* issue of the nineties. In every major city, there are daily reports of street crimes and violence against persons: attacks on joggers in parks, on patrons of parking garages and people who ride public transit; abductions of students in school yards and stalking of coeds on college campuses; muggings of worshippers in churches and of tourists in hotels and resort areas; and mass shootings of patrons in fast-food restaurants and in workplaces. The accumulation of daily incidents reported by the media in lurid detail creates the illusion that no one is safe, no place is safe when even the places traditionally associated with refuge and retreat—our homes, neighborhoods, and workplaces—become the scenes of violence and threat.

Signs of the times are new words that have entered our vocabulary to designate new crimes of personal violence. "Wilding" was coined to describe the vicious attack on a woman jogger by a gang of youths in New York City's Central Park. "Drive-by shootings" describe the random shootings of pedestrians from passing cars. "Carjackings" are auto thefts involving personal violence against the car owner. "Swarming" describes the collective action by a gang of youths to steal clothing from individuals or stores in shopping malls. These new forms of personal violence are characterized by their randomness and their violation of public space in urban areas. These crimes, and the fear they instill, are not associated only with large urban areas. They are becoming more commonplace in suburban and smaller communities.

Urban crime and increasing levels of fear of crime are situated within a culture of violence. In popular culture, there is an increase in crime obsession. This includes the prevalence of crime reenactment television shows and hit movies such as *Falling Down* which portrays an ordinary middle-aged man who loses his job, snaps in freeway traffic, and proceeds to go on a shooting spree. A rash of "slasher" films portray women as victims who are stalked by homicidal men. Within the music subculture, rap music is a genre as obsessed with violence as earlier musical genres were with sex. A new video game aimed primarily at children, "Mortal Combat," aims to kill human targets. The repetition of violent imagery desensitizes us to violence and increases levels of fear of crime.

The growth of the drug culture, not just in center cities or in poor neighborhoods, but in suburbs and boardrooms, has spawned a culture of violence and increasing numbers of desperate drug users who will do anything to get drugs. Whole neighborhoods have been taken over by drug dealers who claim for themselves streets, parks, and playgrounds. In some cities gang violence has destroyed any semblance of public life or livability. In Los Angeles, where an estimated 1000 gangs have 150,000 members, there were 270 gang-related homicides in 1993.[1] Lax gun control laws have put guns into the hands of criminals and make it legal even for children to possess weapons in some U.S. states. A decade of government cutbacks, economic restructuring, increasing poverty and homelessness, have fueled the growth of a large underclass with no hope of participating in mainstream society. All these forces, and many more, have contributed to the building of a culture of violence that is now playing itself out in cities.

There is a perception that violent crime is on the increase. Homicide is often used as a reliable indicator of violent crime because it is uniformly reported. Most recently violent crime has taken an upswing. Between 1986 and 1990, homicides rose by 14 percent in the United States.[2] In 1990 the homicide rate nationally in the United States was 9.4 victims per 100,000 inhabitants.[3] A 1991 U.S. Senate judiciary committee report puts these statistics in an international perspective. The U.S. murder rate is three times that of Canada, four times that of Italy, and nine times that of England. The report concludes that the United States is the most violent of all industrialized nations.[4]

These national statistics actually hide the far higher crime rates in major U.S. cities. In just one city, New York, in 1992, there were 1,995 homicides and guns were used in 75 percent of the city's homicides.[5] Not everyone is equally at risk: Homicide rates are five times higher among blacks than among whites and the rate among Native Americans is almost double that of the rest of the U.S. population.[6]

Violent crimes such as forcible rape and aggravated assaults have increased far more than homicides. In the United States, in the period 1981 to 1990, there was a 24 percent increase in reported forcible rapes, with a 12 percent increase from 1986 to 1990. Aggravated assaults showed an increase of 59 percent between 1981 and 1990, but a 26 percent increase in the period 1986 to 1990.[7] Forcible rapes and aggravated assaults increased by 2 percent in 1992. This reflects 108,730 reported forcible rapes and 1,114,600 aggravated assault victims who reported the crime.[8]

While these statistics may reflect a higher level of reporting of such crimes as sexual assault in the past few years, they also support public perceptions that violent crime is on the increase. People may also be reacting to actual crime rates as they experience them rather than official statistics. Official statistics on rape rates in the United States substantially underrepresent the true rape rates which are estimated to be between three and 20 times as high as official statistics.[9] National crime surveys conducted in conjunction with the U.S. census have found that the largest U.S. cities have the greatest number of rapes.[10]

FEAR OF CRIME

In urban areas, fear of crime is as much a problem as crime itself and is an important policy issue in its own right. Fear of crime is often associated with fear for one's personal safety, especially safety from violent crime and harassment in public when alone, especially after

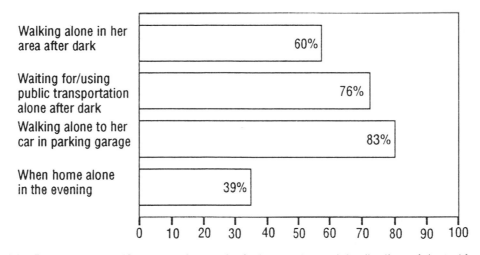

Figure 1-1. Percent women 18 years and over who feel worried in certain situations. Adapted from Statistics Canada. *The Violence Against Women Survey*, "The Daily" Catalogue No. 11-00 1E. November 18, 1993.

dark. Women's fear of violent crime is associated with fear of sexual violence. Fear of crime keeps people off the streets, especially after dark, and out of parks, plazas, and public transit. It is a substantial barrier to participation in the public life of the city.

Fear of crime is unequally distributed. In the 26 largest United States cities, six out of ten women said they felt unsafe in their neighborhoods at night. Women were twice as likely as men to report feeling unsafe. The most vulnerable women felt most unsafe: women of color and widowed, separated, divorced, and older women.[11] Women with disabilities are highly vulnerable and at risk from sexual assault.[12]

Women tend to be most fearful in urban public spaces. In a recent national study of 12,300 women over the age of 18 conducted by Statistics Canada, six-in-ten women were fearful walking alone in their neighborhood at night. Walking alone to a car in a parking garage generates the highest level of fear, followed by using public transportation after dark. Even staying home at night generates fear.[13] Women worried most about such unavoidable situations as going to the laundromat, using public transit, and walking by bars, parks, or empty lots.[14]

For many women these are necessary activities that they must engage in on a day-to-day basis. Women often limit their activities because of fear of crime: They stay home at night; they don't take night courses; they don't go to the grocery store; they don't visit friends or socialize. Many women will not take jobs that keep them out at night. As a response to fear of crime a large number of women isolate themselves in their own homes. Increasingly these homes are barricaded and fortified to keep out criminals. Recent studies have shown that women use a wide range of defensive behaviors to cope on a day-to-day basis with fear of crime. [15] According to Margaret Gordon and Stephanie Riger,[16] "Those women with fewer financial, educational, and personal resources—the poor, the elderly, blacks, Hispanics, and the less educated—relied even more than the average woman on these especially restrictive tactics to protect themselves." Women will drive rather than take transit or walk despite "green policies" to reduce traffic congestion and air pollution. They prefer surface parking lots to underground parking structures, even though many cities are eliminating surface lots in favor of more efficient land use. Women will stay out of certain parts of the city, often downtowns, at night, or they will not use community programs that are scheduled at night. Sometimes these behaviors are seen as irrational or self-indulgent by urban planners and designers, but they make perfect sense as a response to women's fear of being sexually assaulted.

Women's self-defensive behavior has real consequences not only for individual women but also for the city as a whole. Fear of crime limits women's access to resources and opportunities, such as employment or continuing education. But it also affects the livability and viability of the city: Fewer people use the streets; city services may not be used by the people who need them; stores in downtown centers may lose customers; and employers have a more limited pool of employees.

Women who live in cities are engaged in an ongoing situational analysis of the environments of daily life. When asked to identify "dangerous places" in the city or in their own neighborhood, over three-quarters of all women name very specific places where they take special precautions.[17] They identify certain streets or alleys, parks, deserted places, public transit, parking garages, and elevators. When asked what it is about the places that makes them feel unsafe, women are very specific: poor lighting, places that are isolated or deserted, and places where there is no access to other people.[18]

Analyses of crime data from Chicago neighborhoods show that women are most sensitive to signs associated with danger and social disorder: graffiti, abandoned buildings, or teenagers hanging out. These are all signs of physical or social incivility and women respond by increased use of precautionary tactics.[19] Women seem to be identifying what criminologists call "hot spots" of predatory crime and fear, places where criminal incidents have occurred or places that a group or community has identified as particularly dangerous.[20] In his studies of plazas and street life in New York City, William H. Whyte found that women are more sensitive than men to cues of social and physical disorder. He concluded that women's desertion of certain public places in cities is a signal, just like the canaries in mines, that the place is in trouble.[21]

Despite the media focus on public violence and attacks by strangers, the most dangerous place, especially for women and children, is still the home. Violence against women takes place primarily in the home, the last refuge for women increasingly fearful in more public spaces. This often results in an escalation and cumulation of fear levels, as women realize that they are at risk everywhere and that no place is safe.

The L.A. riots and race riots or youth riots in other major cities focused fears that have been building about increasing violence in cities. No matter how inaccurate the focus on street crime, the bottom line is that *everyone* is more scared in public places. The right to enjoy public spaces in the city has been eroded, and may, in some places and for some people, be lost.

TWO APPROACHES TO CONTROLLING URBAN CRIME: LAW AND ORDER AND ROOT CAUSES

There have been two predominant approaches to controlling urban crime.[22] The most prevalent response has been to call for greater law and order: more police, tougher laws, stiffer jail sentences, and keeping people in jail longer. The assumption is that crime and fear of crime result from too many criminals and insufficient criminal justice. The second approach has been to focus on root causes of crime: systematic disadvantage, neglect, and discrimination. Proponents of this approach argue that the affluent 1980s created wealth and prosperity for some but governments ignored the growth of groups that were permanently left out, people who now have little stake in the social order or in public civility. The solutions are viewed as training and education, job creation, economic development, and job creation in poorer communities.

A typical law and order response was U.S. President Bill Clinton's 1993 anti-crime initiative which proposed to spend $3.4 billion over five years to put an additional 50,000 police officers on the streets. New York City's new crime initiative put 3000 more police on the streets. "Project Safety L.A.," the response to the L.A. riots, promised to hire an extra 2000 police officers at an estimated cost of between $100 million and $300 million.

Yet the police cannot maintain public order. They cannot deal with the pervasive unease generated by litter, disorderly behavior, or horrible crime events. The vast majority of the population living and working in major cities cannot be so protected and insulated that they will be safe from purse snatchings on the streets, muggings in the subway, or sexual assaults in parks and other public spaces.

Paradoxically, the law and order response creates a police state. Mike Davis describes this as the "Fortress L.A." phenomenon.[23] Police barricade and seal off poor neighborhoods as part of the war on drugs. Attempts to secure the city result in the destruction of public space used by the poor and homeless. This includes forced removals of homeless people from public parks such as Tompkins Park on New York City's Lower East Side, elimination of such urban amenities as public toilets, or urban design that makes sleeping impossible in bus shelters. In these ways, the safety of public areas and access to public space by a diversity of users are becoming very politicized issues.[24]

Institutions have responded by increasing private security, turning their office buildings into modern fortresses through the use of video cameras and other new security technologies. This has made the private security industry one of the fastest-growing service industries in North America. In the United States, the ratio of private to public police is 2.5:1; in California, it is 4:1.[25] Annual growth of the security industry in the 1990s is forecast to be upwards of 15 percent.[26]

Other privatized solutions also respond to the decline in public safety. Shopping malls and residential enclaves of gated communities surrounded by security walls and policed by private security guards serve the affluent in our society. The poor have nowhere to shop as companies pull out of high-crime areas. Urban residents are lured to small towns and villages by the promise of freedom from fear. At an individual level the 1990s trend of "cocooning" is, in large part, a flight response engendered by higher levels of fear in urban environments.

Privatization of public space and private security are short-term and limited solutions.

Only the privileged few can surround themselves with private security guards; only a small number of people have the option to move to rural areas or small towns. The cities and their satellite communities will continue to provide the employment and services for the majority of the population. Many people living in cities have few choices: They cannot choose where they live, shop, or go to school. Many people are dependent on public transportation. They are forced to survive on a daily basis in high-crime areas.

Nor can people retreat to the suburbs and beyond and expect to be protected from crime. The suburbs increasingly have many of the same problems as center cities: Violence against women and children is endemic behind the closed doors of suburban communities. Despite the limited public realm in suburbs, youth crime, centered on shopping malls and plazas, is on the rise.

The large-scale abandonment of the public realm as a response to fear of crime impoverishes us all. It means the abandonment of the streets, the plazas, the parks, the public libraries, the commercial strips, the public schools, places open by right to all citizens. It means the replacement of public access with private spaces that can be controlled by security guards and the ability to pay.

Dividing responses to violent crime in cities to an attack on either root causes or increasing law and order has paralyzed governments and citizens alike. Solving crime problems through dealing with their roots in poverty, economic restructuring, or systemic discrimination is a long-term strategy that will require massive injections of money and cooperation among all levels of government and all sectors of the community. At a societal level, there are few signs that this is likely to occur.

Certain communities have made commitments to work on root causes of violence, but the resources available to these efforts fall far short of what is devoted to policing initiatives. In Los Angeles, for instance, church groups have designed a crime prevention program that will finance 22 teams of outreach workers to try to steer kids away from gang recruiters in tough neighborhoods. Approximately $5 million has been allocated for this effort compared with at least 20 times that amount for additional policing.[27]

At an individual level, people view the complexity of the root causes of crime and despair at the possibility of positive change. They respond by retreating or feeling so helpless in resolving the problems of crime in their communities that they give up.

Although the predominant response to the increase in violent crime in U.S. cities is to increase policing, there is no evidence to suggest that law and order approaches or fortress-building responses deal adequately with the problem of increasing public violence. We do not know that putting more police on the street or that heavier sentencing will reduce crime. We do not know whether the proliferation of personal safety devices will protect people or whether adding barbed wire and brick walls will keep people safe. The paradox is that the law and order response kills the city it is purporting to save. It deepens the divisions and the fear of the "other" which are among the most harmful effects of fear of crime.

SAFER CITIES INITIATIVES:
THE THIRD ALTERNATIVE

There is an alternative to the law and order and fortress security approach that is gaining in popularity in Britain, the Netherlands, France, Germany, and Australia. This is the Safer Cities approach, an approach to urban crime that encourages partnerships among national governments, cities, neighborhoods, and citizens. The functions of national Safe Community initiatives, in countries where they exist, are to amass and share information between projects, evaluate projects, create models of "good practice," and distribute national funds to the local level. In Canada and the United States, there are city projects that can easily be described as Safe Community initiatives, but no real national clearinghouse exists as yet.

The European and British initiatives provide examples of what national programs can accomplish. In the Netherlands, a 1985 national policy paper on "Crime and Society" created a National Inter-ministerial Crime Prevention Committee with a budget of U.S.$25 million over five years. The money was disbursed to local governments for projects that emphasized the prevention of criminal behavior among youth through education and job creation, self-defense for girls and women, and giving downtown businesses the hardware and community support to fight property crime. The major focus of the crime prevention committee, however, was preventing fear of crime in cities through adequate information and surveys, and a mixture of design and community development improvements to housing estates, transportation systems, and city centers. Many of the participating cities, such as Amsterdam, Eindhoven, and Almere, focused on women's perceptions of unsafe places and their suggestions for change. The committee also publishes a quarterly magazine updating projects and creating a national data bank on crime prevention initiatives.

In Britain, the Safer Cities Programme provided funding in its first year, 1989–90, to 16 local projects in England, as well as separate funding to seven projects in Scotland and Northern Ireland. The local projects have followed a plethora of directions: everything from physical security for homes, business, and public buildings to schemes aimed at encouraging reporting and providing support to victims of racial harassment; from funding "women's safe transport" companies to improving playgrounds on public housing estates; from hiring counselors to work with abused Asian women to hiring a security officer with an electric buggy for a twelve-story parking garage. The British Safer Cities Programme publishes a magazine that summarizes new ideas and has also established a computerized information network.

France has a National Crime Prevention Council that channels funds from the national government to the state and local levels. In 1987, there were 21 such contracts between the national and local level and an estimated 500 local crime prevention councils had been set up. However, the French program lacks both the scope and the funding of the British and Dutch initiatives.

In 1988, Australia established a National Committee on Violence, producing a report, *Violence: Directions for Australia*. A conference on Local Government Creating Safer Communities in late 1991 seemed likely to result in a national funding and information-sharing program.

New Zealand's Crime Prevention Unit, located in the prime minister's office, is funding the creation of Safer Community Councils nationwide. In Canada, the federal government convened a consultation process and conference on a national strategy for community crime prevention in 1992. The proposal is to establish a National Crime Prevention Council that would serve as a vehicle for developing and designing community-based initiatives to prevent crime and devise strategies to deal with its root causes.[28]

In the United States, the national crime prevention strategy seems to consist primarily of funding to put more police on the streets and to create community boot camps for young offenders. The kind of coordinated support for city crime prevention programs found in

European Safer Cities initiatives happens only on an ad hoc basis. In a recent *New York Times* article, Stephen Goldsmith and Kurt L. Schmoke,[29] the mayors of Indianapolis and Baltimore respectively, argued eloquently for an increased federal role in community crime prevention that supports local solutions. They urged the federal government to coordinate federal resources in projects and to provide seed money to local projects, evaluating the results and disseminating them more widely.

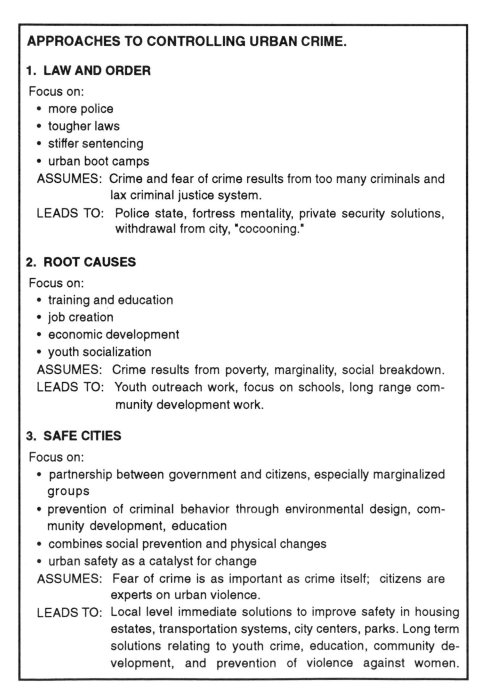

APPROACHES TO CONTROLLING URBAN CRIME.

1. LAW AND ORDER

Focus on:
- more police
- tougher laws
- stiffer sentencing
- urban boot camps

ASSUMES: Crime and fear of crime results from too many criminals and lax criminal justice system.

LEADS TO: Police state, fortress mentality, private security solutions, withdrawal from city, "cocooning."

2. ROOT CAUSES

Focus on:
- training and education
- job creation
- economic development
- youth socialization

ASSUMES: Crime results from poverty, marginality, social breakdown.

LEADS TO: Youth outreach work, focus on schools, long range community development work.

3. SAFE CITIES

Focus on:
- partnership between government and citizens, especially marginalized groups
- prevention of criminal behavior through environmental design, community development, education
- combines social prevention and physical changes
- urban safety as a catalyst for change

ASSUMES: Fear of crime is as important as crime itself; citizens are experts on urban violence.

LEADS TO: Local level immediate solutions to improve safety in housing estates, transportation systems, city centers, parks. Long term solutions relating to youth crime, education, community development, and prevention of violence against women.

Figure 1-2.

WHAT CAN CITIES DO?

Some cities have taken the initiative to fight crime and mobilize community action. Cities like Amsterdam, in the Netherlands; Toronto, Canada; and Manchester, England, act as a catalyst and model for fighting crime. The city of Toronto, for example, developed a focus on municipal strategies to prevent violence against women which committed the city, and almost every city department, to developing urban safety initiatives. City Council set up a Safe City Committee with members drawn from community organizations and politicians. The city's Official Plan was changed to include urban safety objectives.

The starting point for the city's crime prevention initiatives was what city departments could accomplish within existing programs and budgets. The Buildings and Inspection department drafted new legislation requiring better security in parking garages and in multiunit housing. The Parks and Recreation Department developed a new policy for security in parks and recreation centers and offered free self-defense classes for women. Public Works developed a program to replace all streetlights with a new energy-efficient, pedestrian-friendly design. The Housing Department studied urban safety problems in its housing projects and began work to make improvements. Within the Planning and Development Department, training programs were developed so that staff could incorporate issues of safety and security. A design guidelines book was published and distributed to all planning staff and other professionals in the development and housing field. These guidelines were adopted by the city council and applied in the ongoing development review process for new projects.

These changes all affected urban safety in the physical environment of the city, especially in public space. They also addressed the issue of civility. By setting and enforcing new standards for lighting and maintenance, the city sent out the message that local government has the responsibility to ensure that public space is safe and actually accessible to the public.

Besides physical changes, the city also focused on projects of social prevention. The Health Department worked with a union to develop an education program for workplaces, concentrating on wife assault. The city provided free self-defense courses during working hours for thousands of its female employees and developed a new program on sexual assault and sexual harassment prevention. Toronto's City Council also strengthened community action by providing $500,000 in funding for community groups fighting to break the cycle of violence against women and by developing resource kits to help organize neighborhood crime prevention.

By providing leadership, seed money, and access to city resources, the city of Toronto illustrates how a city-based crime prevention strategy works. Public consciousness that citizens can do something positive to combat urban crime and that the city will support them in their efforts is very high. New initiatives in the schools, by the business community, in specific neighborhoods, or by special interest groups, for example cyclists, sprout up regularly.

The city of Toronto is not unique in its approach. In Nottingham, England,[30] a crime audit determined the financial costs to the city of crime and fear of crime in the downtown area. Changes involved improved lighting and security in parking, and setting up safe women's transport. Funding was provided to small shop owners and residents of public

Figure 1-3. City agencies can work to educate the public to prevent violence. The Toronto Transit Commission and police department jointly produced this bus shelter ad against gay bashing. (Photo: Gerda Wekerle)

housing to improve security. Local action plans were targeted to preventing youth crime and to improving the safety of women and the elderly. An interagency working group focused on racial harassment and set up a project to combat racial violence. Safe Cities funds also supported the probation service in its crime prevention role and set up a police-run prevention shop in the city center.

Other British cities have provided free installation of locks for the elderly and have improved public security in parks, railway and bus stations, shopping centers, hospitals, and schools. These changes encouraged better use of public facilities and served to strengthen communities. Safe Cities projects have placed a high priority on women's safety and the safety of ethnic groups, as well as developing youth programs in schools and communities. Multiagency partnerships and partnerships between citizens and local governments are the driving force behind such projects.

In U.S. cities, there are many local initiatives that have not received much attention. In Baltimore's Sandtown neighborhood, a high-crime area, the city government and residents worked together to suppress the drug trade. Changes included the construction of new housing and jobs for residents to build the housing. Improvements in city services included

Figure 1-4. Community rally to stop drug traffic on New York City's Lower East Side, March 1988. The rally ended in front of Mayor Koch's West Village apartment. (Photo: Marlis Momber)

road work and family counseling. In Houston's Link Valley area, where cocaine use was a problem, police provided security for a neighborhood cleanup that involved working with city officials and landlords to secure vacant buildings, and finding developers to invest in the area.[31] In St. Paul, Minnesota, the city has developed a program targeted to decreasing domestic violence, funded community organizers to work with neighborhood groups to reduce crime, passed a new bylaw to improve security in parking garages, developed a design ordinance for urban safety, and funded a design guidelines manual to promote urban safety. The city also supports a community policing initiative. In Chicago, The Chicago Alliance for Neighborhood Safety, a coalition of more than 30 neighborhood organizations, developed a community policing proposal for the city. Boston's Safe Neighborhoods Program focuses on curbing gang violence. The city increased beat patrols by police, hired street workers to counsel teenagers in high-crime neighborhoods, and created 8300 summer jobs for youth and programs to help single parents cope.[32] Due to the absence of a national crime prevention strategy or coordination at the city-wide level, these citizen initiatives are often ad hoc and very localized.

A hallmark of the Safer Cities programs is that solutions are custom-designed to local problems. Communities and citizens are recognized as the experts on urban violence in their day-to-day lives and are seen as the best people to develop solutions. The city provides an enabling framework within which citizens can develop collective solutions. Rather than giving up or retreating into privatized cocoons, citizens start with their concern and fear for themselves, their families, homes, neighborhoods, and workplaces. Often these initiatives come from the most marginalized groups in society: women, racial and ethnic minorities, the elderly, and the poor—the people most at risk from urban crime. Many initiatives start out small and local. Citizens begin by looking at the environments of their daily lives, proposing micro-changes that will decrease their fear of crime. These are the places where improvements are immediately felt. By starting with community initiatives, the city develops multiple strategies to control crime. Law enforcement is only one such strategy. Initiatives to fight fear and prevent crime are also given priority.

As citizens have achieved some measure of success in making their local parks, housing projects, or schools safer, they have also realized that their involvement has changed the politics of urban safety. They have redefined *what* constitutes a safety problem by focusing on fear of crime as well as crime rates. They have addressed violence against women, instead of limiting the focus to property crimes or drug-related offenses. They have redefined *who* is to be involved in urban safety policy-making. Citizens have also changed the process of who implements changes. Instead of leaving crime to the police and justice system, Safer Cities initiatives involve a multitude of actors making small decisions and changes in the microenvironments of daily life.

Where they have been tried, Safer Cities programs have demonstrated that a city can create a climate where the whole community makes urban violence a priority. Cities have facilitated partnerships among citizens, government agencies, and the police to come up with locally based solutions. By providing a focal point for initiatives and a tool kit of resources and information, the city acts like yeast that starts other community initiatives growing. Most importantly, Safer Cities initiatives provide a different perspective on urban safety. Instead of defining crime as a problem of policing and the justice system, Safer Communities programs redefine urban safety as part of the public policy agenda that is integral to all aspects of urban life.

Crime Prevention Through Environmental Design

Cities involved in crime prevention initiatives often start with the built environment. They recognize that our buildings, streets, open spaces, and parks are not merely the settings in which crime occurs but that the fabric and design of public places can deter criminal activity and enhance urban safety. Crime Prevention Through Environmental Design (CPTED) is one approach to the design and management of urban space to reduce the incidence and fear of crime. It involves detailed situational crime analysis to identify localized patterns and the microenvironmental conditions that might be creating opportunities for crime to occur. This entails close observation of urban space as it is used and attention to the social and cultural definitions of how it should be used.

Crime Prevention Through Environmental Design was introduced in the early 1970s. Architect Oscar Newman's book, *Defensible Space*, popularized an approach that linked crime reduction and prevention to design changes. Alice Coleman, a British geographer, is a well-known proponent of CPTED in Britain. Both Newman and Coleman focused on improving urban safety in public housing projects. Newman's work emphasized the critical importance of informal surveillance of areas, especially through visual accessibility. He also focused on ways to increase a collective sense of responsibility for common areas. Coleman has emphasized the importance of addressing signs of incivility, including graffiti, and controlling access through fences and locks.

This early work has spawned a veritable CPTED industry, with a diploma course provided by the National Crime Prevention Institute, University of Kentucky, Louisville, and the spread of the CPTED concept to police forces and private security consultants. Reduced to a small number of strategies and approaches, the CPTED approach is often marketed as a simple, easy-to-use technique that reduces crime prevention to primarily a design problem that can be applied to all situations and environments.

Critics of the CPTED approach argued that causal links between defensible space modifications and reductions in crime had never been demonstrated.[33] They pointed out that design never operates independently of wider social and management factors. Newman and Coleman both focused on public housing environments. Their emphasis on creating a sense of territoriality and controlling access to strangers by cutting up common space or privatizing it, cannot be applied to urban public spaces that must be accessible to large numbers of people. Early CPTED initiatives also did not deal with fear of crime and the substantial variations of fear of crime found among different groups. CPTED focused primarily on reducing property crimes; there was no acknowledgment that violent crime prevention in urban public space might require different measures. The association of CPTED with outside experts, architects, security consultants, or police, who would analyze the built environment and make recommendations for simple, physical, one-time-only changes, was attractive to property managers or building owners, but tended to alienate tenants and community residents. This approach ignored the need to build community and involve key stakeholders in developing solutions to crime prevention and in implementing them in the long term.

Crime Prevention Through Environmental Design has become newly popular as the concern with crime and urban fear in cities escalates. Safer Cities approaches often incorporate CPTED. Environmental design strategies are one approach used to reduce site-specific crime and fear of crime. Changes to the microenvironments of daily life are most immediately felt by individual citizens and have the capacity to engage communities in crime prevention. Beginning with changes to the physical environment, communities very directly address the breakdown of physical and social civility that is a product of urban decay and is experienced as a breakdown in municipal guardianship of the public realm.

There is a shift in focus, however, from traditional CPTED approaches. The Safer Cities approach stresses management and community crime prevention, along with design amelioration. Fear of crime is viewed as important as crime levels, as it affects people's behavior and the general livability of the city. There is an acknowledgment that in a climate of wariness and fear, people practice defensive environmental use and they scan the environment more for site-specific factors that make them feel unsafe.[34] Crime prevention strategies focus on all environments, not just housing environments, and not just environments used by poor people or minority groups. There is a concentration on the needs of those who are most vulnerable—not only women, but older people, people with disabilities, and lower-income people. There is a new focus on partnerships—between the public and private sectors; between community groups, local government, and the police in defining problems and in implementing solutions. There is a recognition that treating people as experts in the problems of their community generates new information and solutions.

DESIGN AND PLANNING GUIDELINES
FOR SAFER CITIES

The guidelines for safer cities presented in this book are tools for environmentally assessing urban public spaces for danger of violent crime. They should be viewed as "possible responses" to specific environmental conditions. They can be used to evaluate specific schemes or to highlight missing features. They may be used to write programs or to initiate discussions with community groups. They are based on our synthesis of existing knowledge in the field and current practice. The guidelines are provocative. They call for a reevaluation of current planning and design assumptions and practices. This may serve to promote awareness and better understanding of urban safety.

The guidelines are organized into checklists that you can quickly review in evaluating a specific space or type of urban environment. The items included in the checklist are to alert you to specific features that may be problematic. As you go through the checklists, you may begin to look at spaces you use in new ways. We encourage you to listen to your own feelings of unease and anxiety in certain places and to try to identify not only why you are fearful there but what kinds of changes would make you feel more comfortable in using such places.

While we have tried to include in this guide the latest information on design, planning, and management responses to violence and urban crime, following these guidelines will not guarantee that a place will be crime-free or that no incidents will ever occur. Every city, neighborhood, and urban space has its unique characteristics that combine physical environment, social relations, and culture. The concepts outlined in this book are only part of a broader crime prevention policy. What works in one community may not work in another. These guidelines give you many starting points and examples of initiatives that have been tried elsewhere. But they are not intended to be the final statement on Crime Prevention Through Environmental Design. While implementing some of these guidelines may reduce the risk of crime, we cannot guarantee results or accept legal responsibility for any costs or consequences arising from or related to their implementation or performance. Practice is constantly evolving as cities and organizations implement specific strategies and assess their impacts on urban crime.

This book focuses on what cities can do and have done to respond to increasing levels of fear of crime and urban violence. We address this book to the professionals who make decisions about urban built form and how it will be used: architects, planners, developers, transportation engineers—people who have not generally been exposed to issues of urban safety in their professional training but are now required to deal with this problem. We also encourage community groups, and especially women's groups, to use these guidelines to look closely at the built form of their cities to identify changes that would make them feel safer in urban environments.

NOTES

1. T. Appleby, "L.A.'s new take on crime," *Globe and Mail* (October 15, 1993), A19.
2. U.S. Department of Justice, Federal Bureau of Investigation, *Uniform Crime Reports 1990* (Washington, D.C.: U.S. Department of Justice, 1990).

3. K. Maguire and T. J. Flanagan, *Sourcebook of Criminal Justice Statistics 1990* (Washington, D.C.: U.S. Department of Justice, Office of Justice Programs, Bureau of Justice Statistics, 1990), 353.

4. Knight-Ridder Newspapers, "U.S. 'most violent' nation Senate crime report says," *Toronto Star* (March 13, 1991). For Canadian statistics see S. Fine, "Growth in violent crime slows in Canada," *Globe and Mail* (August 31, 1993).

5. G. James, "Crime down in New York for 2nd year in row," *The New York Times* (March 19, 1993).

6. Associated Press, "U.S. found most violent of industrial nations," *Toronto Star* (November 13, 1992) (citing a National Research Council report).

7. U.S. Department of Justice, Federal Bureau of Investigation, *Uniform Crime Reports 1990* (Washington, D.C.: U.S. Department of Justice, 1990).

8. Associated Press calculations based on FBI Uniform Crime Report. Associated Press, "Murder rate in U.S. down 6%, FBI reports," *Toronto Star* (April 26, 1993).

9. M. T. Gordon and S. Riger, *The Female Fear* (New York: Free Press Books, 1989), 33.

10. Gordon and Riger, 33.

11. Gordon and Riger, 9.

12. L. Stimpson and M. C. Best, *Courage Above All: Sexual Assault Against Women With Disabilities* (Toronto: DisAbled Women's Network, 1991).

13. Statistics Canada, *The Violence Against Women Survey, The Daily*, Catalogue 11-00IE, November 18, 1993.

14 Gordon and Riger, 14.

15. Gordon and Riger, 16–17.

16. Gordon and Riger, 114.

17. Gordon and Riger, 12.

18. Gordon and Riger; B. Sterner, *The Women in Safe Environments Report* (Toronto: Women Plan Toronto, METRAC, Faculty of Environmental Studies, York University, 1987).

19. Gordon and Riger, 112–117.

20. J. L. Nasar and B. Fisher, "'Hot spots' of fear of crime at the micro and macro scale," Paper presented at the 23rd Environmental Design Research Association Conference, Boulder, Colorado, April, 1992.

21 W. H. Whyte, *The Social Life of Small Urban Spaces* (Washington, D.C.: The Conservation Foundation, 1980).

22. S. Goldsmith and K. L. Schmoke, "Crime control, city by city," *The New York Times* (December 19, 1992), 23.

23. M. Davis, *City of Quartz: Excavating the Future in Los Angeles* (New York: Vintage, 1992), 223–263.

24. K. Franck, personal communication.

25. R. Titus, National Institute of Justice, Washington, D.C., personal communication.

26. "Going to market," *Security Management* 34 (1990), 84–87.

27. T. Appleby, "L.A.'s new take on crime," *Globe and Mail* (October 15, 1993).

28. Department of Justice, Canada. *Consultation Document: National Crime Prevention Council* (Ottawa, January 1994).

29. Goldsmith and Schmoke, 23.

30. Home Office, *Safer Cities: Progress Report, 1989–1990* (London: Home Office Crime Prevention Unit, 1990).

31. Goldsmith and Schmoke, 23.

32. C. Sullivan, "U.S. cities using curfews to curb teen violence," *Toronto Star* (April 15, 1991).

33. F. Stoks, *Assessing Urban Public Space Environments for Danger of Violent Crime: Especially Rape*

(Seattle: Ph.D. Dissertation, Department of Urban Planning, University of Washington, 1982); "Assessing urban public space environments for danger of violent crime, especially rape," eds. D. Joiner et al., *Conference on People and Physical Environment Research* (Wellington, N.Z.: Ministry of Works and Development, 1981), 331–42; B. Hillier, "In defence of space," *RIBA Journal* 8, 11 (1973), 539–44; B. Hillier and J. Hanson, *The Social Logic of Space* (Cambridge: Cambridge University Press, 1984); R. B. Taylor, S. Gottfredson, and S. Brower, "The defensibility of defensible space: a critical review and synthetic framework for future research," eds. M. Gottfredson and T. Hirschi, *Understanding Crime: Current Theory and Research* (New York: Sage, 1980); M. Jenks, "Housing problems and the dangers of certainty," eds. N. Teymur, T. A. Markus and T. Woolley, *Rehumanizing Housing* (London: Butterworths, 1988), 53–62.

34. Nasar and Fisher, 1992.

2

The Process of Planning
for a Safer City

Making cities safer is a complex and time-consuming process. It is much easier, and probably more useful, to begin by describing how *not* to plan for a safer city. This is a somewhat exaggerated, but nonetheless accurate example:

Newspapers and television stations in Dystopia City have been giving much coverage to a "crime wave" in one of the city's rougher neighborhoods. Dystopia City Council, which has never before considered how its public spaces might be made safer, votes to bring in an International Expert at enormous expense. The International Expert spends several hours peering at the neighborhood through the haze of jet lag, accompanied by a planner and two academics who generally avoid the area. "Aha!" the Expert proclaims, "It is as I thought. Knock this apartment building down. Put a road through this housing project. Increase the wattage of these street lamps by 10 lux each, and call me in the morning."

This kind of quick fix, top-down, cookie cutter formula has been resorted to all too often. The effects can do more harm than good to the people whom the plan intends to help. The problems of any city/neighborhood/park/building are probably complex and took a long time to get that way. The solutions must also admit complexity and be thought of in the long term.

GOALS AND PRINCIPLES

Because planning for a safer city is so complex, it is more useful to think in terms of three general *goals*:

First, there must be an **awareness** of the issues by people with authority, and a commitment that these people with power have a positive role to play in mitigating crime and fear in urban environments. Second, the **processes** must be created whereby existing urban environments are improved, and new urban environments planned with safety in mind. Third, **mutual learning** must be set in place, whereby evaluation of these improvements is continually taking place, and ideas are expanded and modified.

The City of Nottingham, England has listed five further design *principles* that guide its Safer Cities project. Although these principles are developed for its downtown core, they have relevance for neighborhood and suburban planning as well.[1]

1. **Design for pedestrians to move about in well-lit, wide-circulation routes that reflect existing patterns of movement.** This principle takes for granted that well-used and vibrant streets are essential for safety. Measures that enhance street life—encouraging street vendors in the downtown, calming traffic in residential neighborhoods—are to be encouraged. Measures that detract from street life—overhead walkways and underground malls in the downtown, houses and shopping centers that turn away from the street in the suburbs—should be discouraged.

2. **Consider safety of people and property together rather than separately.** In traditional Neighborhood Watch and Business Watch schemes, it is assumed that people are more concerned about robbery than personal safety. This was never true for women, and is becoming less true for men. Police, planners, and shop owners are coming to the realization that street crime, assault, and harassment may be less "visible" than broken windows and stolen property, but have higher economic and social costs.

3. **Use opportunities for enhancing natural surveillance.** As in the first principle, the underlying implication is that caring neighbors and strangers are the best defense against assault. However, not only should parks, pathways, and parking lots allow people to see and be seen, but ways of helping yourself or getting help should be clearly indicated as well.

4. **Good maintenance.** Good maintenance is crucial for design improvements to continue being a success after their implementation. Adding lighting in apartment stairwells does no good if it is allowed to stay burned out; a fence that is broken no longer fulfills its function. This principle reminds us that design improvement is not a one-shot event, but rather a continual process, and that "design" encompasses social factors as well. Places should also be designed for easy maintenance, without resorting to the extreme of a "defensible" yet sterile environment.

5. **Make sure solutions to one problem don't create another.** Perhaps the most important design principle, it reminds us that safety must be factored into decisions. Will the environmental benefit of turning off the lights in a parking lot after 10 P.M. outweigh its negative impact on personal safety? When considering safety, this principle also encourages thinking about a space in its context. Will fencing in a playground make it more of an entrapment spot?

THE BASIC PROCESS FOR CONSIDERING URBAN SAFETY IN SMALL PROJECTS

Keeping these principles in mind, there is a basic *process* that all projects, no matter how small, should go through. At the very least:

1. **Every development proposal should consider the impact its design might have on the safety of its users and on the surrounding neighborhood.** If the architect and developer have not dealt with this aspect, then it is the responsibility of the planner and other local officials to bring it up. If community groups raise concerns, they should be listened to.

2. **If actual or potential users are consulted—and this should be encouraged— then personal safety should be explicitly considered in these discussions.** The basic questions that need to be asked are:

   a. How do/would you use this space during the day and evening?

   b. Have you encountered personal safety problems in this space or a space like this? Have these concerns been dealt with? How should they be dealt with?

   c. Do any specific parts of this proposal seem unsafe? How might they be improved?

Safety audits of the neighborhood can raise issues and promote constructive ideas. Simplified plans can also be reviewed by potential users or other concerned community people.

Discussion will not be limited to design issues. Police–community relations, community crime prevention, and the provision of community services often are raised in consultations. Sometimes these points have design implications, which should be noted. Other comments can be noted and passed on to appropriate bodies.

3. **Some record of how safety concerns were dealt with should be kept, in order to develop a knowledge base.** Planning reports should include a section on safety concerns. Developers and architects should keep records on how plans were modified for safety reasons, including drawings and photographs. Regular peer meetings can be used to share experiences.

A SUGGESTED PROCESS FOR MORE COMPLEX PROJECTS

What if the plan is more complicated than a single apartment building? Let's say that you are a planner charged with drawing up a neighborhood improvement plan. Or you are working for a community organization that is planning a new center. Or you are an architect, commissioned to create a downtown park. A *four stage process* is suggested.

Stage One: Thinking It Through

Ask yourself certain questions, in order to understand the parameters of the project to be undertaken, and the resources on hand:

1. **Where is the area to be improved?** Is it as small as part of a building, or as large as a new neighborhood? Is it in a low- or high-income neighborhood, or

is it mixed? Likewise, is the population homogenous in terms of culture or language? If not, are there mechanisms to involve all on an equal footing?

2. **Why is this process occurring?** Is it in response to a particular crime or series of crimes? This may be good: The urgency may translate into money and people being assigned. This may be bad: Quick fix solutions will be expected.

3. **Who is initiating the improvement?** Has the idea of improving a park, housing project, neighborhood, or downtown core come from the users of this space? This may be good news: The necessary energy and information may be there for the asking. This may also be bad news: Lack of money resources or power may soon frustrate users.

   Has the idea come from the owners of the apartment building or downtown stores? Good: They may contribute money. Bad: Their views may differ from the users, or they may be frustrated by lack of cooperation from the local powers-that-be.

4. **Who will be affected by the improvement?** Many people or few? A diverse group of people, or a unified group? What are the potential conflicts? Who needs to be consulted?

5. **Who should be involved in directing the change?** A small group may be more efficient, a large group more representative. Typical people to involve in a reference group include:

   planners/community developers
   police and other law enforcement officials
   architects/developers
   residents or tenant associations
   Neighborhood Watch or other community safety groups
   groups that represent a constituency: women, racial and ethnic minorities, youth, older people, people with disabilities
   local politicians and other decision makers
   shopkeepers or owners of commercial properties
   drop-in and community centers

Involving key stakeholders means more than checking plans with a neighborhood political leader. If a large number of disabled or elderly people are affected, it would make sense to consult a group representing these interests. Likewise, since women are more affected by violence and fear of violence, it is important to aim for gender parity and to involve any local women's groups (even if the group is as "informal" as a parent/child drop-in).

Also note that assembling a reference group does not obviate the need to consult separately with the larger population.

6. **What people resources are on hand?** How often should a reference group meet? Are there paid staff associated with this project? Can volunteers be remunerated in some way (certainly for child care, transportation, and meals)? Do volunteers have time to consult with their communities?

7. **What money resources are on hand?** Can an existing rail station or park be completely rebuilt? Is there money for new staff or expensive hardware such as video cameras? Or is the budget limited to lights and mirrors?

As you will see in the examples used in this book, money is rarely the most important element of a successful project.

8. **When is the project expected to be completed?** How long are the people— staff and volunteers—and the money available? What needs to be done by the date of completion?

Stage Two: Gathering Information and Developing Options

Now that you have embarked on the project, you need to choose a plan of action. Questions to be asked include:

1. **The "facts".** Collect not only police statistics about crime in the area, but additional information, if possible, from rape crisis centers and other sources. Remember that sexual and other assaults are usually grossly underreported, and accept that anecdotal information may be the most accurate source of crime incidence and fear of crime.

2. **The story thus far.** Have there been crime prevention or other related initiatives associated with this area? Are they considered successful or unsuccessful? Can the successes be built upon? Can the failures be avoided?

3. **Learning from experience.** What kinds of concerns have been expressed about similar places in the past? What kinds of solutions were developed? Did they work?

4. **Consultation.** Aside from the reference group, who else will you consult with? At what stage will you consult? Most importantly, how will you consult?

The timing and length of meetings, the accessibility of a location, and the legibility of site plans and written materials should all be considered when consulting with community people. For instance, you may attract more parents with young children if you pay for child care, more older people if you provide some assistance with transportation and do not go on too late, more people with disabilities if you ensure that the meeting location is wheelchair accessible and sign language interpreters are provided. Rather than expecting people to come to you, you may go to existing groups such as tenants' organizations or ethnospecific agencies.

Remember to consult the occasional as well as the usual users of a space. For instance, the signs in a parking garage under an office building should be designed to direct people who are parking for the first time as well as the everyday user.

5. **Deciding on a mechanism for evaluation.** How and when will you decide success or failure? Will you use one or a combination of : crime statistics, user satisfaction, a poll on fear of crime, increased use of space? You may wish to take "before" pictures of the site at this point.

At the end of the second stage, there should be a recommended plan of action or choice of actions and a timetable, as well as background information (preferably summarized in written form).

Stage Three: Choosing and Carrying Out the Plan

You have developed recommendations, now it is a matter of carrying them out.

1. **Making the final decision.** Is this the responsibility of a reference group? Do you need another community meeting to decide? Does the final decision rest in the hands of the local council or the developer? Are last-minute modifications acceptable?

2. **Publicizing the changes.** Quite often, it is important to publicize the changes as they occur. For instance, if a new emergency button system is being installed, people must know where to find it and how to use it. If a pedestrian pathway is being rerouted, the new route must be made absolutely clear.

3. **Keeping construction sites safe.** (fences locked, detours well lit) is also vital.

4. **Constant monitoring.** Are new ideas cropping up that can be incorporated? Is it already clear that a change is not working, or is working very well? Can these ideas and concerns be dealt with before the changes are final?

When construction is complete and the reference group disbanded, there is still the all-important last stage.

Stage Four: Evaluating the Plan

1. **Carrying out the evaluation.** Who will carry out the evaluation—an independent observer or one of the actors in the process? Are the evaluation mechanisms decided upon at the beginning of the process still valid?

   One of the most important questions in any evaluation is whether the change supported individuals and communities or whether it contributed to fragmentation and bad feeling.

2. **Making modifications based on the evaluation.** Have you used your evaluations and feedback to improve the project or process for the next project?

3. **Keeping a record.** If at all possible, write a report or at least keep the planning materials in one place, in order for you and others to learn from the experience.

A SUCCESS STORY: MELBOURNE'S WEST END FORUM

A successful example of a process that used many of these principles is the West End Forum in Melbourne, Australia. The West End Forum was created in June 1990, as a result of a recommendation by the state body set up to improve safety, the Victorian Community Council Against Violence. Melbourne's West End is a typical "seedy" downtown area, the home of the city's major nightclubs and most of its hotels as well as rooming houses and small businesses (including licensed houses of prostitution). The particular crimes being addressed were violence in and around licensed premises—the nightclubs and bars—but a broader approach was taken.

The Forum consisted of representatives from residents' groups, the Center Against Sexual Assault, the nightclub industry, the Australian Hotels Association, the police, the Liquor Trades Union, and the Victorian Community Council Against Violence. A full-time project officer was hired for one year, using state funds. The Forum was divided into five subcommittees: planning and design, traffic and bylaws, venue management, policing, and transport.

Over the course of a little over a year, the Forum conducted safety audits of the area, leading to significant improvements to area parking lots and changes to the Official Plan. Nightclub managers made training and education available to their employees and developed a code of practice that dealt with the workers' own safety as well as preventing harassment. A complaints committee was also instituted for the self-governance of the clubs. New signs and pamphlets publicized the changes in the nightclubs. Police created foot patrols, and the rooming house tenants and small businesses formed associations to assist in their concerns. At the end of the Forum's mandate, a report was written by the project officer. While it was perhaps too soon to evaluate in terms of reduced rates of violence, certainly all the participants felt that the area had been made safer and there was a new sense of community responsibility.

Perhaps the most remarkable feature of the West End Forum is how it brought together disparate groups for a common purpose. Prostitutes and police officers participated in the safety audits. Nightclub owners, traditionally seen as part of the problem, realized that providing an intimidation-free space was in their best interest. Design and management changes were planned and implemented using a truly representative consultation process.

COMMON PROBLEMS

As most people who have participated in the process of planning for a safer city know, the ideal of disparate groups coming together to work towards a common goal is rarely easy. Some *common problems* include:

1. Getting the Process Started

Whether you are an office worker concerned about your workplace, a housing developer anxious about community resistance to a nonprofit project, or a planner working in a department that has not yet taken personal safety concerns seriously, raising safety issues is often the hardest part of the process.

Resistance to including personal safety concerns often takes one or more of these forms:

> **"It will cost too much".** The cost of decreasing crime and fear of violence is almost always less than the direct and indirect costs of crime. Most of the ideas and strategies in this book are low cost and low maintenance. A variant of this is:
> **"If we deal with safety and someone is assaulted, it may make us liable".**
> Housing projects, transportation companies, universities, and businesses have

successfully been sued by people who have been assaulted in these spaces be-cause they have been shown to be negligent by not taking sufficient steps to make them safe.

"It doesn't work". This book is full of successful examples of planning, design, and management improvements. As mentioned above, success should not only be measured by crime statistics, but also by user knowledge and satisfaction, the number and variety of users, and equity considerations such as increasing the comfort levels of women, the elderly, and visible minorities.

"It is all too much to deal with". Because safety audits are low cost, concrete, and easy to do, they are often a good first step in dealing with concerns.

2. Dealing with Conflict

Conflict is almost inevitable when dealing with such emotionally charged subjects as crime and violence. Conflicts usually arise on one of two subjects:

What has priority? Are aesthetics or environmental concerns more important than safety? This is often reduced to such absurd and false choices as "If we deal with safety in this park, we'll end up by paving it" and "If we light everything, we will contribute to the greenhouse effect." The answer often lies in taking a deep breath and considering these concerns as complementary rather than conflictual. Obviously, a paved park isn't a solution: A combination of well-signposted more- and less-active areas may be. Improving lighting standards may result in more energy-efficient as well as more pedestrian-focused lighting.

When concerns are not complementary, it makes sense to put safety first. Placing parking areas in hidden-away lots may be more visually pleasing, but it no longer makes sense in the urban context.

Who has priority? A city's planning department says routing public roads through a large housing project will help integrate it in the city; the tenants oppose it. A resident's association says adding a shelter for battered women will make the neighborhood less safe. A women's group asked to come up with a renovation of a commuter rail station recommends grade crossings instead of the existent overhead walkways; the railway says that this is impossible because of cost and traffic safety.

Assuming compromise is impossible, and recognizing that each situation is unique, the following principles might be kept in mind:

People who will be using a space should be listened to more than people who won't.

People who are more vulnerable should be listened to, rather than the people with the loudest voices.

In order to reduce such conflicts, the parameters of a project (including cost and whether a project can be rejected) should be established from the beginning.

3. Evaluation

You may not know, especially in the short-term, whether an improvement is working or not. Involving a community in an assault prevention project may inflate crime figures because people may feel comfortable reporting assault for the first time. Adding two-way radios or emergency alarm buttons in a public transit system may win plaudits from women's groups and individual transit travelers, but fear of crime may still increase due to external factors.

Evaluation can be based, instead, on the following factors:

Do users know about the improvement and do they approve?

Do more people know what (new or previously existing) safety features are available and how they are used?

Are there more people using the space?

Even if you are dissatisfied with the indicators of improvement, it is still important to give an honest evaluation.

BEYOND INDIVIDUAL PROJECTS

Looking beyond individual projects to larger policy changes, the following ideas would benefit safety in cities:

1. **Set up municipal safety initiatives.** Safer Cities programs have blossomed in recent years in the United Kingdom, Canada, Australia, and New Zealand. Minneapolis and St. Paul are probably the first cities in the United States to consider this model. The programs bring together local politicians, police, civil servants, and community groups to tackle crime and violence issues in a comprehensive and cooperative manner.
2. **Include safety in official plans.** Municipalities in Canada, the United Kingdom, and Australia have incorporated wording in their official plans that mandates including safety in plan review.

In Toronto, the most recent Official Plan now includes the following statements:

3.20 Safety in Design

Council shall promote safety and security in public places, including street, parks and open spaces, schools, public transit and public parts of building. To encourage public safety and security for all persons, but with particular attention to women, children and persons with special needs, Council will:

a) ensure that public safety and security are important considerations in City approvals of buildings, streetscaping, parks and other public and private open spaces;

b) encourage the design and siting of new buildings to provide visual overlook and easy physical access to adjacent streets, parks and open spaces, and to allow clear views to parks and open spaces from the street;

c) improve existing streets, buildings, parks and other publicly accessible areas, where existing conditions do not promote public safety and security; and

d) require appropriate lighting, visibility and opportunities for informal surveillance for parking lots and garages.[2]

Council has adopted the use of guidelines for urban safety in plan examination.[3]

7.20 Planning for a Safer City

It is a goal of Council to promote a City where all people can safely use public spaces, day or night, without fear of violence, and where people, including women and children and persons with special needs, are safe from violence. Accordingly, Council shall adopt development guidelines respecting issues of safety and security and shall apply those guidelines in its review of development proposals.[4]

3. **Training on safety issues.** Whether shared among municipalities, limited to a particular department such as parks or building inspection, or bringing together campus building and maintenance people, workshops on planning for a safer city are a necessity. The issues discussed in this book are rarely part of the curriculum in professions such as architecture, landscape architecture, and urban planning, and this too needs to change. The Association of Professional Engineers of Ontario has embarked upon the development of training materials on public safety for its 50,000 members. In Ottawa, Canada, a Safer Places Network consisting of the regional planning department; the local chapters of the architects, landscape architects, and planners' associations; the Women's Action Centre Against Violence; and the Crime Prevention Council of Ottawa have organized a series of professional development workshops on planning and safety topics.

4. **Action research.** Action research on the places where vulnerable groups, especially women, feel unsafe, and ideas for improving these places have been successful in a number of cities. Toronto's *Women in Safe Environments (WISE) Report*[5] was the result of cooperation between a university, a community-based women's organization, and an agency. Manchester's report on women and safety came from its planning department. Ottawa, Canada, and Eindhoven, Holland, included surveys in their local newspapers to gather information.

   This research needs to make special efforts to include the perspectives of visible minority and disabled women. The Greater London Council made a point of hiring visible minority women to interview other Asian and black women for its survey on women and transportation.

   Research that expands the traditional parameters of "planning for a safer city" is also growing. The Metro Toronto Action Committee on Public Violence Against Women and Children (METRAC)'s recent work on Ontario campuses includes harassment issues and touches on questions of management and curriculum.

5. **Sharing information.** In countries where Safer Community programs are being established, the linkages among these programs is still weak. Australia

recently held a conference on Local Governments Creating Safer Communities. The British Safer Cities program publishes annual progress reports and a bimonthly publication, *Crime Prevention News.* The European and North American conferences on Community Safety and Crime Prevention (there have been four since 1985) also provide occasions to share experiences and ideas, but a computer network or some other more regular mechanism for international exchange would be useful.

6. **Evaluation.** Independent evaluation of crime prevention projects, from small sites to city-wide initiatives, is still a rarity. Much more work needs to be done on the criteria for evaluation, especially the measures of success or failure. These evaluations also need to be shared within and between cities.

Wendy Sarkissian, an Australian planning consultant, has spoken of the essential first step in the process of planning for a safer city: opening our hearts to the fear, and then moving away from the denial of violence.

NOTES

1. Nottingham Safer Cities Project, *Community Safety in Nottingham City Center* (Nottingham, U.K., 1990).

2. City of Toronto, Official Plan Part I, Adopted by Toronto City Council (June 21, 1993).

3. Planning and Development Department Staff (Carolyn Whitzman) and Gerda Wekerle, *A Working Guide for Planning and Designing Safer Urban Environments* (Toronto: City of Toronto, Planning and Development Department, 1992).

4. City of Toronto Official Plan Part I, June 21, 1993.

5. Metro Action Committee on Public Violence Against Women, Women Plan Toronto and Faculty of Environmental Studies, *Women in Safe Environments* (Toronto: METRAC, 1987).

3

Factors that Enhance Safety and Security in Public Space

This book divides urban safety into three areas: awareness of the environment, visibility by others, and finding help. Incorporating these planning and design factors enhances safety and security by offering opportunities to escape from the "moving crime pattern."

1. **Awareness of the environment** means that the design and layout of a place is understandable. This includes the ability to see and to understand the significance of what is around and what is ahead—through adequate lighting, clear sightlines, and elimination of entrapment spots—in order to avoid dangerous situations.

2. **Visibility by others** means that a person using a building or space will not be isolated. This includes the ability to be seen, through reduction of isolation; improvements to the mixture and intensity of land use; and intelligent use of activity generators.

3. **Finding help** means that a person can receive assistance from others. This includes the provision of clearly marked avenues to assistance such as emergency exits, alarms, and phones and the ability to escape, communicate, or find help when in danger, through improved signage and legible design.

AWARENESS OF THE ENVIRONMENT

Lighting: The Problem

After dark, fears of personal violence and risks are heightened for both men and women. Badly designed and poorly lit areas offer opportunities for crime to occur and give the message that an area is uncared for. Poor lighting is not the main reason most assaults in public places occur at night; it is because of other factors such as normal time of socializing, alcohol use, movement to and from work, and scarcity of people.[1] However, improving lighting decreases fear of crime and levels of interpersonal crime, as a recent study conducted in Britain found. After improved lighting was installed in a badly lit street and tunnel, 62 percent of residents felt safer and the number of incidents was dramatically reduced.[2] This study argues that:

> If good lighting increases the risks that offenders may be recognized or increases the chances of someone coming to the aid of a victim who has been attacked then it deserves more attention as a preventive strategy than it has hitherto received.

Improved lighting encourages people to use public places at night and may increase informal, natural surveillance. As a community crime prevention strategy, good lighting improves the look of areas, encourages people to use the streets, contributes to a sense of personal security, and is often low cost.

In the typical North American city, streetlights hang over the middle of the street, lighting cars that are provided with headlights. The sidewalk is rarely lit, even though this is the area that needs lighting. Some cities have retained their 19th-century pedestrian-oriented lighting; other cities are trying out new lighting designs that will light the sidewalk and not the middle of the street.

Public spaces should be lit for pedestrians, not just motorists. The level of lighting in public spaces must be adequate to have a good look at another person when he or she is still a reasonable distance away. This basic level of lighting is often not met. In 1988, when Toronto's Safe City report was published,[3] 75 to 80 percent of Toronto's street lighting was below the illumination standard of 4 footcandles set by the Canadian Standards Association.

A commonsense way to look at the level of lighting is to ask "Are you able to identify a face 15 meters/yards away?" The ability to have eye contact with a person you are about to pass at a reasonable "flight" distance is a common measure of security. Keep in mind that seniors and those with decreased vision will need an increased standard of night lighting.

Not only the level of lighting, but its consistency, may be a problem. Many public transit users report the temporary blinding effect of passing by a flood-lit bus shelter onto an under-lit street. Often, the lighting glares toward the person approaching, making it impossible to see that person. Alleys, inset doorways, and other potential hiding spots adjacent to well-traveled routes sometimes have no lighting at all.

Overlighting and inappropriate use of lighting can be a problem. For instance, a person who lights the perimeter of a property so that the light shines into a neighbor's home is hindering informal surveillance rather than helping it. In general, it is preferable to provide more fixtures with lower wattage than a few with higher wattage.

Lighting alone will not make a place safer. Lighting the first part of a path leading into a wilderness area, for instance, may contribute to a false sense of confidence in the user that the area is frequented or policed at night. Lighting isolated spaces, such as wilderness paths, may give a false impression that the path is well used in evening hours and a false sense of security.

The replacement of incandescent lighting with high-pressure sodium lighting is occurring in several North American and European cities. This dramatically improves lighting levels and results in significant energy savings but in some cities there are debates about the aesthetics of sodium lighting.

Lighting: What to Look For

(Check the items that apply to each site.)

MINIMUM STANDARDS

☐ If the place is intended to be used at night, can you identify a face 15 meters/yards away?

☐ Are pedestrian pathways, laneways, access routes in outdoor public spaces lit to the minimum standard of 4 footcandles? This should include alleys or laneways and other inset spaces, access and egress routes, and signage.

CONSISTENCY OF LIGHTING

☐ Is lighting consistent, i.e., with few or no areas of shadow or glare, in order to reduce contrast between shadows and illuminated areas?

PROPER PLACEMENT OF LIGHTING

☐ Does street lighting shine on pedestrian pathways and possible entrapment spaces rather than on the road?

☐ Are inset doorways, alcoves, and above- or below-grade entrances lit?

☐ Does lighting take into account vegetation, including mature trees, and other potential blocks?

☐ Can store owners be persuaded to mount lights on stores to increase pedestrian-level street lighting?

Figure 3-1. Pedestrian scale lighting on Montreal's St. Denis Street (Photo: Gerda Wekerle)

Figure 3-2. New light standard, combining easy maintenance with attractive design in a Toronto social housing project (Photo: Vincenzo Pietropaolo)

Figure 3-3. Combining lighting for cars and pedestrians in Toronto's financial district (Photo: Gerda Wekerle)

MISLEADING LIGHTING

☐ Are paths or spaces not intended for nighttime use unlit to avoid giving a false impression of use?

PROTECTION OF LIGHTING

☐ Are light fixtures protected from casual vandalism by such means as wired glass or a lantern-style holder?

MAINTENANCE

☐ Are lighting fixtures maintained in a clean condition and promptly replaced if burned out or broken?

Development agreements should state who is responsible for maintenance of lighting. A public notice indicating who to call in case of burned-out or vandalized lights helps maintain lighting fixtures.

PLANNING FOR NIGHTTIME USE

☐ Do architectural drawings or development proposals reflect nighttime conditions, including use and the position, quantity, and type of lighting?

Sightlines: The Problem

The inability to see what is ahead along a route because of sharp corners, walls, earth berms, fences, bushes, or pillars is a serious impediment to feeling and being safe. The ability to see what is ahead and around is known as "visual permeability."

Of special concern are large columns, tall privacy fences, overgrown shrubbery, and other thick barriers adjacent to pedestrian paths which could shield an attacker; impermeable landscape screens and long fences that serve to cut off access to means of escaping a place; and elements such as insets adjacent to paths which could serve as entrapment spots. Low hedges or concrete planters, small trees, wrought-iron or chain-link fences, transparent reinforced glass or plastic, lawns or flower beds, benches and lampposts all denote boundaries while allowing users to see and be seen.

Routes may be planned with closed views in order to add "interest" to a building or public space. Grade separation and landscape screens are also used for their aesthetic value; to provide private outdoor space; to shield "unpleasant" buildings, parking lots, and car traffic. Conflict over right-of-way may lead to odd jogs in tunnels and pathways. While total visual permeability is not always possible, the above motives for blocking sightlines should be measured against potential personal safety effects. Grade separations, where building entrances are either above or below grade, block sightlines, especially when landscaping or walls are added.

Fire regulations may create limitations to secure design. For instance, double doors in parking garages help control the spread of fire but create two points where the person cannot see what is beyond a door.

Users should be able to see where they are going to make reasonable choices of routes. Creating spaces and pathways with good sightlines also means that users are visible to others who can come to their assistance.

Sightlines: What to Look For

(Check the items that apply to each site.)

SHARP CORNERS

☐ Are sharp "blind" corners avoided, especially on stairs or in corridors where movement can be predicted?

☐ Can sudden changes of grade that reduce sightlines on pathways be avoided or changed to allow for sightlines.

HIDDEN ENTRANCES

☐ Are entrances to housing units hidden or inset?

PERMEABLE BARRIERS

☐ Are barriers along paths, for example fences, visually permeable?

ESPECIALLY PROBLEMATIC PLACES

☐ Is special care for sightlines taken into account in spaces where risk to personal safety is perceived to be high?

Figure 3-4. In-fill housing, Minneapolis, Minnesota. Entrances are hidden by high walls and staggered, making it difficult for informal surveillance by neighbors. (Photo: Gerda Wokorlo)

□ Are there good sightlines in stairwells of parking garages?

□ Are there good sightlines in lobby entrances to high-rise buildings?

□ Is the office or superintendent's apartment located near the building entrance?

□ Are there good sightlines to laundry rooms or apartment storage areas?

IMPROVING SIGHTLINES

□ In spaces or paths where sightlines are impeded, can hardware such as security mirrors be added to make it easier to see?

□ Can laundry rooms or storage areas be moved to areas of higher activity, e.g., adjacent to a front door or in a courtyard?

The best security mirror is a ceiling-to-floor shiny aluminum angled mirror. Convex mirrors of either aluminum or shatter-resistant glass can be provided in corners as an alternative.

LANDSCAPING

□ Will the choice of landscaping materials serve as screens or barriers to an unimpeded view along pathways when they mature?

□ Do landscaping, berms, or structural features impede views into playgrounds, small parks, or plazas located adjacent to the sidewalk?

Entrapment Spots: The Problem

Entrapment spots are small, confined areas, adjacent or near a well-traveled route, that are shielded on three sides by some barrier, such as walls or bushes. Examples are elevators, storerooms, fire stairs, dark recessed entrances that may be locked at night, gaps in tall shrubbery, curved or grade-separated driveways, or loading docks off a pedestrian route. Parking lots, gas stations, and used-car lots can become entrapment spots, especially when adjacent to pedestrian routes. Hidden areas adjacent to school buildings or isolated school yards may also be entrapment spots, especially at night. Below-grade or above-grade plazas may create places that are isolated or invisible from the street.

Figure 3-5. A full-length polished aluminum mirror provides an excellent view around this corner in a Toronto subway station. (Photo: Toronto Transit Commission)

Figure 3-6. At this high-rise building, the laundry room (with open window), is located adjacent to the front door, providing passive surveillance by laundry room users and making them feel safer while doing their laundry. (Photo: Sandra Colangelo)

Figure 3-7. This vest-pocket park in downtown Toronto offers an urban oasis while preserving good sightlines into the park. Notice the well-chosen and well-maintained vegetation. (Photo: Vincenzo Pietro-paolo)

Figure 3-8. This fountain, without water, with its high brick walls, cuts off sightlines at an intersection beside Washington, D.C.'s Convention Center. (Photo: Gerda Wekerle)

Figure 3-9. Gaps in the street may create entrapment spots. An entrance to an interior courtyard of a college creates an environment that is private and isolated after dark. This was the site of a nighttime sexual assault. (Photo: Gerda Wekerle)

Entrapment Spots: What to Look For

(Check the items that apply to each site.)

ENTRAPMENT SPOTS ADJACENT TO PEDESTRIAN ROUTES

☐ Is there an entrapment spot(s) adjacent to a main pedestrian route, e.g., storage area, hidden area below or above grade, or a private dead-end alley?

☐ Can it be eliminated?

☐ Can activities be added, e.g., food kiosks or vendors?

LIMITING ACCESS

☐ Can the area be closed off-or locked in off hours? For instance, can the stairwell to a locked building be locked as well?

☐ Are there dead bolt locks for storage areas off pedestrian routes?

☐ Is there limited access to loading docks or other restricted areas?

LIGHTING AND SIGHTLINES

☐ If an entrapment area is unavoidable, is it well lit?

☐ Are there aids to sightlines such as convex mirrors?

Figure 3-10. A classic assault site. A movement predictor (stairwell leading to the entrance of a shopping mall and subway station), with an entrapment area below grade (an unusable and unattractive plaza invisible from the street). (Photo: Vincenzo Pietropaolo)

☐ Are potential entrapment areas covered by video cameras?

☐ Are there regular patrols of isolated stairwells and storage areas?

Movement Predictors: The Problem

A movement predictor is a predictable or unchangeable route or path that offers no choice to pedestrians. An assailant can predict where persons will end up once they are on the path and can lie in wait for them. The obvious example is a pedestrian tunnel, but narrow passageways, pedestrian bridges, moving sidewalks, and staircases also serve as movement predictors. Movement predictors are of particular concern when they are isolated or when they terminate in entrapment spots.

Tunnels are not necessarily dangerous per se, although they are almost always noted as places that are feared. However, a frequent stranger assault scenario involves an assailant meeting a victim in a tunnel, then taking her to a nearby dangerous place using force. Due to concerns about personal safety in tunnels, Amsterdam, in the Netherlands, and Manchester, England are no longer building pedestrian underpasses to speed car traffic. Instead, they are designing safer level crossings.

Figure 3-11. Spaces between buildings on New York City's Upper West Side are gated and fenced to prevent them from becoming entrapment spots. The razor wire, while possibly a deterrent, adds to the sense of physical incivility. (Photo: Gerda Wekerle)

Figure 3-12. Locking potential entrapment sites after work hours makes the street safer for pedestrians. (Photo: Gerda Wekerle)

Figure 3-13. This bus shelter in Washington, D.C., is open along one side so that users cannot be trapped inside. Advertising does not obscure views into the shelter. (Photo: Gerda Wekerle)

Movement Predictors: What to Look For

(Check the items that apply to each site.)

ELIMINATION OF MOVEMENT PREDICTORS

☐ Can a movement predictor, e.g., a tunnel, passage, bridge, or staircase, be eliminated, rather than attempting costly improvements?

☐ Do pedestrians have optional routes?

SIGHTLINES

☐ Can a pedestrian see what is in a tunnel and what is at the end of it?

Installation of full-length stainless steel mirrors, when the tunnel has a corner, or transparent doors to an entrance may help.

LIGHTING

☐ Is lighting adequate and consistent, avoiding pools of shadow?

☐ Is natural lighting possible?

☐ Do wall and ceiling materials reflect light?

While natural lighting of a tunnel helps reduce its "endless night" quality during the day, it must be supplemented during nighttime hours, if open.

Figure 3-14. Overhead and underground walkways were popular in the 1960s and 1970s, and are still regularly proposed today. In almost every case, pedestrians would rather take their chances with cars. This walkway links City Hall Square with the Sheraton Center, Toronto. (Photo: Vincenzo Pietropaolo)

Figure 3-15. Pedestrians using this overpass in San Pedro, California, can see and be seen but the design reminds people of a cage with no opportunity for escape. (Photo: Roger Keil)

HARDWARE

☐ Can emergency telephones, intercoms, or video cameras be added?

☐ Is the means to summon help well-signposted?

ALTERNATIVE NIGHT ROUTE

☐ Is there an alternative well-lit and frequently traveled route that can be indicated at the entrance?

While underground tunnels in the downtown district may be preferable during the day, an alternate route for evenings and weekends might be signposted at the entrance.

JUXTAPOSITION OF MOVEMENT PREDICTOR AND ENTRAPMENT SPOT

☐ Is there an entrapment spot or isolated area within 50–100 meters/yards of the end of the movement predictor?

☐ If so, can it be modified?

Visibility by Others: The Problem

In order for people to feel and be safe, it is vital that they know that people who might help are "keeping an eye on them." A site may well be avoided if it seems desolate, if people

Figure 3-16. This long staircase in St. Paul, Minnesota, is a movement predictor. A person using it has no option but to go up or down and an assailant can wait at the top or bottom. (Photo: Mary DeLaittre)

Figure 3-17. The routes from subway and commuter rail stations often become assault sites used by assailants following their victims from the train. This walkway to train tracks in London, England, is hidden and not well lit. (Photo: Gerda Wekerle)

judge that signs of distress, like yelling for help, will not be seen, heard, or responded to. This, in turn, will make the place seem and be more unsafe. Land use decisions of past decades have created isolated spaces. Nineteen sixties high-rise apartment tower blocks are surrounded by open space that is often neglected and viewed as belonging to no one. Low-density suburban residential developments, with pedestrian pathways and cul-de-sacs, create streetscapes with no people or activities, especially during the day. Large shopping plazas turn inward away from the street, and drain the streets of vitality. Their large parking lots are isolated at off-peak hours and increasingly become sites for abductions, assaults, and carjackings.

Police and other security personnel provide formal surveillance, but cannot see all places at all times. In a recession, security personnel or parking attendants may be cut back in number or be poorly trained. Informal surveillance from adjoining commercial and residential buildings may help mitigate the sense of isolation, as does planning for a greater intensity and variety of use.

In some especially dangerous or isolated spots, there may be the need for formal surveillance in the form of audio monitors, video cameras, or staff. But it is important not to overrely on formal surveillance hardware: A video camera, aside from its cost, will only help if there is a twenty-four-hour attendant who knows what to do in a dangerous situation and who can be supervised to ensure that surveillance takes priority over reading the paper. In some cases, one person is expected to monitor up to 40 screens, too many to watch all day. Hardware can also easily be vandalized and take long periods to repair.

Visibility by Others: What to Look For

(Check the items that apply to each site or situation.)

INFORMAL SURVEILLANCE

☐ Do building windows overlook pedestrian routes?

☐ Are blank facades avoided at street level?

☐ Are bus stops placed near areas of activity rather than in isolated areas?

☐ Can new uses be introduced to isolated places through in-fill developments?

ESPECIALLY PROBLEMATIC ROUTES

☐ Are routes to and from parking lots or garages overlooked?

☐ Are routes clearly marked so that users can exit quickly and by the most direct route?

INCREASING ACTIVITIES AND USE

☐ Can a concierge be provided in an apartment lobby?

☐ Can isolated spots in malls or transit stations be animated by vendors or street entertainers?

☐ Can programming activities increase off-hours' use?

HARDWARE

☐ Is there a telephone, emergency telephone, or alarm and is it adequately signed?

☐ Are isolated areas covered by video cameras?

☐ Are staff who monitor video surveillance equipment trained to respond to emergencies?

Figure 3-18. A suburban bus stop that is isolated in a no-man's-land with no adjacent activities. At night, bus passengers waiting at this stop would feel very vulnerable. Suburban bus stops are often sited beside empty fields, ravines, gas stations, or by themselves. (Photo: Toronto Transit Commission)

Figure 3-19. Isolated walkway connecting a subway station and bus platform under the new Century Freeway, Los Angeles. Passengers have no alternative route. (Photo: Roger Keil)

Figure 3-20. This downtown parking lot in Toronto benefits from the surveillance provided by windows from an adjacent town house complex. (Photo: Gerda Wekerle)

Figure 3-21. A hot dog vendor at a walkway to a commuter rail station informally keeps an eye on this path, as well as providing an amenity to the commuter on the run. (Photo: Vincenzo Pietropaolo)

Land Use Mix: The Problem

Separating industrial, institutional, retail, and business uses from each other and from residences creates public streets that are unused at particular times of the day and evening. More indirectly, it is difficult to create a sense of community when people use a neighborhood to do only one thing, whether it be to sleep, play, work, or shop. Recent years have seen a return to the principle of land use mix for environmental and social reasons. But good land use mix is also important for safety reasons.

An example of how land use separation contributes to fear of crime is suburban planning of the post-war period. A bus might stop along an arterial road, with shopping strips and high-rise apartments set back far from the street and parking lots in the forefront. In order to enter the low-rise residential area, the transit user might have to use a pedestrian pathway bounded by planting and fences, or take a circuitous and equally isolated set of under-lit streets. This is hardly a model of planning for safety.

Land use mix cannot be considered without taking scale into account. Beyond a certain scale of height and size, which is partly dependent on the scale of the surrounding neighborhood, residents and workers lose touch with the street and with other developments. A high-rise office tower cannot be expected to provide informal surveillance of the street; even if workers can see to the street, the view to nearby buildings and the skyline will hold more interest than the ant-like figures far below. A development will seem fortress-like to user and nonuser alike if it is big enough and not scaled to its users and to the environment around it.

The positive health, environmental, and economic effects of smaller-scale developments are being recognized as cities develop Main Streets initiatives to increase the density of commercial strip developments by adding three or four stories of housing above stores. The model is New York City and older European cities like London and Paris. New developments are aiming to intensify uses in suburbs through such Main Streets projects. Large-scale in-city redevelopment projects such as Battery Park in New York City intersperse financial, commercial, and residential uses.

The answer to problems caused by land use separation and large-scale single-purpose areas has often been to mix and intensify land uses. But mixed uses must be compatible with one another and with what the community needs. For example, adding a school or a community center to the edge of an already isolated area may not increase safety of that area. Adding higher-income housing to a low-income housing area without the community's consent may not increase safety. Adding one housing project to an office area may not be fair to the people who will live in this potentially isolated and under-serviced location.

Land Use Mix: What to Look For

(Check the items that apply to each site or situation.)

COMPATIBLE MIXED USES

☐ Are there compatible mixed uses that encourage activity, informal surveillance, and contact among people during the day and evening?

Examples include services, workshops, and stores in primarily residential areas, especially if they provide local employment opportunities, and child care centers and grocery stores

Figure 3-22. Broadway on New York's Upper West Side is a typical mixed-use area. Apartments above stores, including food stores, drugstores, coffee shops, meat markets, bookstores, and movie theaters, ensure pedestrian traffic at all hours. (Photo: Gerda Wekerle)

in office areas. The advantages of adding services to office areas include the possibility of adding residential uses at a later date.

☐ Are there mixed uses that add to users' fear of crime or increase risk?

Combining a large commercial parking garage with residential uses may require careful attention to security and separation of uses.

BALANCING "NEGATIVE" LAND USES

☐ How might nearby land uses considered negative be balanced by positive measures?

Bars, video arcades, and areas of street prostitution are inevitable elements of urban life, no matter how much some residents may be made uncomfortable by them. The question is how other land uses might be added or modified that would help address the discomfort.

☐ Would the bar be less of a prominent feature of the street if there were more restaurants, or if its outdoor advertising was toned down?

SCALE

☐ Is the scale of development consistent with its neighbors?

This is important for design reasons, in order to avoid large gaps in the street. But it is equally important for social reasons, in order to avoid the new development being considered as an eyesore by the neighbors.

Figure 3-23. Even the core area of Almere, a new town in the Netherlands, has housing integrated with businesses. This helps to ensure a constant flow of people and eyes on the street. (Photo: Carolyn Whitzman)

Figure 3-24. When mixed use goes wrong. Housing combined with a parking garage establishes the grounds as a place for cars, not people. Residents must cross the parking lot to gain entrance to the housing and the garage brings in a constant stream of strangers. (Photo: Vincenzo Pietropaolo)

Activity Generators: The Problem

Active, vital urban spaces that attract diverse groups of people are perceived as safe places. But many urban spaces lack a sense of activity and liveliness. Activity generators include everything from increasing recreational facilities in a park, to placing housing in a previously commercial area, to adding an outdoor café to an office building. They can include, on a small scale, mixing land uses, but also can include intensifying a particular use. Generating more activity often involves planning for different uses and users rather than design changes. The purpose of activity generators is to add "eyes" to the street or open space; to make a place more secure by populating it.

Activity generators do not operate in isolation. It is not enough to add housing to a commercial area if the housing is isolated and without services. Placing a hot dog vendor in a huge parking lot will only make the hot dog vendor scared.

Activity Generators: What to Look For

(Check the items that apply to each site or situation.)

COMPLEMENTARY USES

☐ Are there complementary uses, especially in potentially isolated areas?

Figure 3-25. A mixture of activities that works. A commercial laundromat is combined with a small video store. The employee's booth allows both to be viewed. Many residents use this staffed laundromat, located across the street from a large public housing project, instead of the unstaffed laundromats in their buildings. (Photo: Vincenzo Pietropaolo)

A children's playground may be located next to a food stand, with a washroom and telephone nearby. A laundry room may be at ground level overlooking a play area, or next to the building entrance or playroom.

COMPLEMENTARY USERS

☐ Are users complementary?

Avoid forcing users to "run the gauntlet" and pass through an area controlled by people considered to be threatening. For instance, locating a play area for younger children next to a basketball court can easily result in the older children attempting to take over the younger children's space. Thinking about who is going to use a space and how they will use it is vital when planning activity generators.

REINFORCING ACTIVITY GENERATORS

☐ Are activity generators located along an "active edge" or along one or two pedestrian paths in large parks or on the boundary of large developments?

An "active edge" creates a boundary of space that is inviting rather than threatening to passersby. Encouraging street vendors or food vendors in parks and the sensitive placement of seating areas informally generates activity along the edge of a path.

Figure 3-26. This entrance to Central Park on Fifth Avenue in New York City attracts street vendors, including a portable bookstall. The result is lots of people and activity. (Photo: Gerda Wekerle)

Figure 3-27. An outdoor café is part of this Amsterdam in-fill housing project. The café faces the rear alley and makes it less deserted. (Photo: Gerda Wekerle)

DESIGN FOR PROGRAMMING ACTIVITY MIX

☐ Do planning and design provide opportunities for enhanced programming, such as cultural and recreational programs in parks or nature walks at night to encourage people to use and "own" the public space?

GRADE-LEVEL ACTIVITY

☐ Are activities located at grade rather than raised off the street or sunk below street level?

☐ Are they turned inward or hidden away so there is limited relationship with the street?

OFF-HOUR USES

☐ Can off-hour uses be developed for potentially dead spaces?

One Manhattan public school uses the school and school yard for a weekly fleamarket. Downtown parking lots can be used for weekend farmers' markets. Carnivals, street fairs, First Night celebrations on New Year's Eve where downtown streets are blocked off and building lobbies are used for entertainment, all bring a diverse population into the streets and enhance the livability of cities.

BRINGING PEOPLE INTO THE STREETS

☐ Can special events be programmed to bring people into the streets, especially after dark in the downtown?

☐ Can space be created for outdoor cafés?

Figure 3-28. A public school in New York city holds a weekly flea market and green market on weekends in the playground and first floor of the school building. (Photo: Gerda Wekerle)

Figure 3-29. On Toronto's Queen Street, T-shirt vendors attract a crowd. The city licenses vendors rather than asking them to move on. The vendors themselves are constant eyes on the street, although too many vendors can create crowding where pickpockets operate. (Photo: Gerda Wekerle)

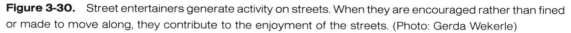

Figure 3-30. Street entertainers generate activity on streets. When they are encouraged rather than fined or made to move along, they contribute to the enjoyment of the streets. (Photo: Gerda Wekerle)

Sense of Ownership/Territoriality: The Problem

Increasing urban safety through design that will encourage a sense of ownership, or territoriality, is controversial. Since the 1960s, public housing projects have been built in large blocks with private streets, walls, and courtyards. Suburban developments have favored physical layouts of cul-de-sacs, private streets, and, more recently, gated communities with gate houses, walls, and limited access points. All these measures are designed to encourage a sense of territoriality among residents so that they will take collective responsibility for the place and for one another and, by extension, act on intrusion. According to architect Mary Vogel:

> When we "own" our communities and take responsibility for our streets, blocks, and neighborhoods, we reinforce the positive efforts of police and other city departments, and our communities are safer, because spaces that are cared for, maintained, and looked after are less likely to be crime scenes.[4]

Designers assume that breaking urban space into smaller spaces shared by a limited number of households will make them accountable to one another and encourage informed social control. Paradoxically, such environments may increase vulnerability to certain types of crime. Enclosed spaces are often underused, isolated, and unintelligible. The primary means by which space is policed naturally may be through the presence of other people.

The solutions are not isolated, enclosed spaces but outward-facing layouts, encouraging access and through routes, and use of public spaces. Attempts to encourage "pride in place" are not dependent on design alone, but relate to the opportunity people have to participate in the design, planning, and management of those places.

The visual or real barriers separating many North American public housing developments from surrounding neighborhoods have created havens for drug dealers and isolated residents from the wider community. Judging from community consultations in Toronto, Canada, London, England and elsewhere, territoriality-inducing measures, such as creating private gardens from open spaces, and decreasing the number of people using an entrance to a building do not work in isolation to reduce crime. These measures are part of a larger set of issues including responsible management, a prompt response to offensive graffiti and harassment, and a safety and security process that truly listens to a community's needs. Not knowing who has formal ownership can be an important contributor to insecurity, since problems such as broken door locks or neighborhood toughs cannot be reported to maintenance or security staff. When public spaces or common areas are vandalized, full of litter, or poorly maintained, users get the message that no one cares. The conclusion drawn is that acts of personal violence might go unobserved as well.

Sense of Ownership/Territoriality: What to Look For

(Check the items that apply to each site or situation.)

SENSE OF OWNERSHIP / TERRITORIALITY

☐ Are courtyards or enclosed spaces overlooked by residences or commercial uses?

☐ Can neighborhood squares provide a focal point for neighboring?

☐ Are activities grouped so that enclosed spaces are not quiet and devoid of life (e.g., play areas, community gardens)?

☐ Are courtyards and gardens locked with keys available only to residents?

☐ Can a grid pattern be created through superblocks by linking streets or expanding pathways?

☐ Can brick walls be knocked down to integrate the isolated, inward-turning housing development with the surrounding community?

☐ Do new building designs fit in with the character of the existing neighborhood?

☐ Can vacant lots be temporarily used as playgrounds, neighborhood parks, community gardens, or fenced off?

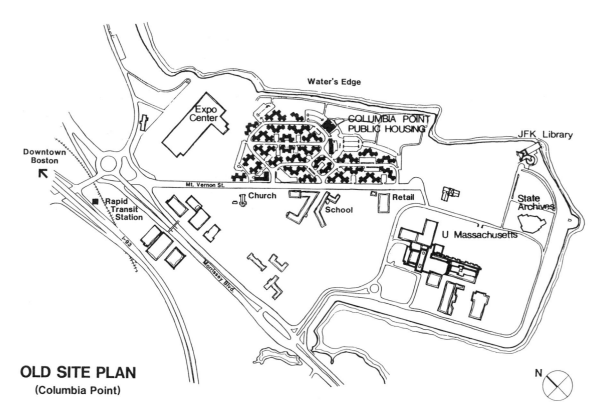

OLD SITE PLAN
(Columbia Point)

Figure 3-31. Columbia Point public housing project, in Boston, is a typical example of the enclosed, inward-turning public housing projects built in the 1960s. It has cul-de-sacs, private streets, block towers, large open spaces that belong to no one, and is cut off from the adjoining community by arterial roads. (Figure: Goody, Clancy and Associates, Inc., Architects)

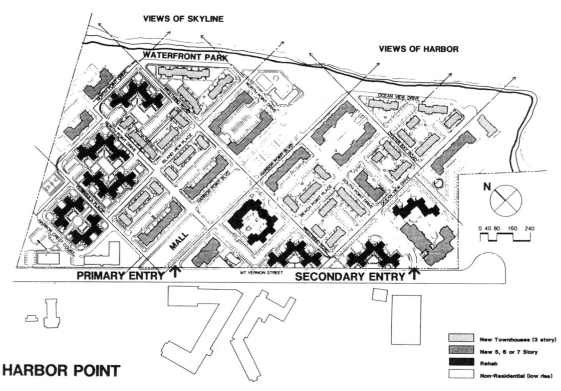

HARBOR POINT

Figure 3-32. A redevelopment plan for the site connects the project to the existing city grid pattern, thereby opening up views of the skyline and harbor. Empty spaces between buildings are filled in with new town houses and low-rise apartment buildings. Existing buildings are rehabbed. The new site plan is more legible and makes it easier for residents and visitors to find their way. The change in name of the project denotes a new image. (Figure: Goody, Clancy and Associates, Inc., Architects)

Figure 3-33. A gated community in Toronto with a gate house staffed by a security guard surrounded by a wall enclosing private streets. The increase in gated communities is a response to fear of crime in large cities. Experience has shown that turning inward has actually increased crime in public housing projects. Relying on security guards and enclosure might be a limited solution to the crime problem for upper-income residents as well. (Photo: Gerda Wekerle)

MAINTENANCE

☐ For a maintenance emergency, such as a broken lock, door, or window, is a phone number to call prominently posted?

☐ Are sexist, racist, and homophobic graffiti promptly removed from walls and sidewalks either by management or by public works if on public property?

☐ On streets, is litter picked up and are repairs responsive and prompt?

☐ Are building occupancy codes enforced to ensure that poorly maintained properties are brought up to standard?

☐ Is there an adequate number of garbage receptacles that are designed to fit into the streetscape?

☐ Is imagination used to solve vandalism problems, e.g., wall murals where walls are subject to constant graffiti; formalizing an informal pathway?

Figure 3-34. Washington Mews, a 19th-century version of a private street near Washington Square in New York City. (Photo: Gerda Wekerle)

Figure 3-35. Bringing activities into a semipublic space is a different strategy. This Amsterdam in-fill project has windows overlooking the courtyard and a pub that draws people from the adjoining community into the space. (Photo: Gerda Wekerle)

Figure 3-36. Racist and sexist graffiti in an Amsterdam housing project leaves a hostile message. Equally disturbing—by not cleaning up these expressions of hate—is the message by the owners of the buildings that they do not care. (Photo: Carolyn Whitzman)

FINDING HELP

Signage and Other Information: The Problem

Knowing where you are and which way to turn contributes to a feeling of security. Public signage is often inadequate, both in amount and quality. What signage there is tends to be of a restrictive nature (e.g., "Don't step on grass," "Do not enter") rather than being actively helpful.

In major cities, one-quarter or more of inhabitants are functionally illiterate; many more are "map-illiterate." Symbols are, for the most part, not standardized, and imaginative responses to these problems continue to elude both the public and private sectors. Graffiti and other vandalism also impede the ability of signs to communicate.

Signage and Other Information: What to Look For

(Check the items that apply to each site or situation.)

SIGN LOCATION

☐ Are signs strategically located at entrances and near activity nodes (e.g., intersections of corridors or paths)?

Figure 3-37. Maps of the neighborhood at all entrances to Paris's Metro stations help orient people so they do not lose their way. (Photo: Gerda Wekerle)

☐ Do they indicate where to go for assistance or help?

☐ Do they indicate where there are telephones?

☐ Do they indicate location of washrooms?

☐ Do they orient users to the nearest busy street?

MAINTENANCE

☐ Do signs indicate how to report maintenance or vandalism problems of the area and of the sign itself?

MAPS

☐ At the entrance to parks, buildings, or building complexes, are there large maps?

☐ In large parks and buildings are take-along maps or leaflets available? (These can be reused by providing drop-off boxes at entrances.)

☐ Do they provide information appropriate to the different needs of various groups of users?

MAIN ROUTES

☐ On the grounds of large buildings, sets of buildings, malls, and parking structures, is the main pedestrian route clearly indicated through maps or floor markings?

☐ Are routes that lead off the main route towards more isolated places indicated as such?

Figure 3-38. Signage at park entrances helps park users to find their way around without becoming disoriented. Central Park in New York City provides large maps at entrances and smaller maps, with lists of park activities for children or joggers, at notice boards in park playgrounds. (Photo: Gerda Wekerle)

Figure 3-39. A pedestrian walk strip in Toronto City Hall's massive underground parking garage helps users find the exit. (Photo: Sandra Colangelo)

Figure 3-40. Signage in parking garages must assist in orienting people to the right exit. This underground garage in the Toronto Dominion Center combines supergraphic street signs on the wall with neon signs orienting users to specific locations. (Photo: Sandra Colangelo)

EXIT SIGNS

☐ Besides exit signs required by law, is other information provided so that users can orient themselves and find their destination (e.g., street designations in underground parking garages)?

☐ Where exits are closed after hours, is this indicated at the entrance to the route?

ALARMS AND PHONES

☐ Are alarms and telephones clearly marked and visible? (Some institutions use a highly visible blue light.)

☐ Are there enough alarms and telephones and are they distributed throughout the space?

Overall Design: The Problem

The legibility and aesthetic value of public and semipublic space contributes to fear of crime or a sense of security. The degree to which users of an area can find their way around, the "legibility" of a space, influences the feeling of security. Legibility has been discussed in the section on signage, but needs to be stressed again as a creator or inhibitor of security. Pedestrians need well-lit paths with clear edges between activity nodes. Good design lessens the need to depend on signs in order to find one's way around.

A barren, sterile environment surrounded with security hardware will reinforce a

Figures 3-41 and 3-42. Emergency call buttons linked directly to building security and public telephones in parking garages give patrons ready access to assistance. Where these are located and how many emergency buttons there should be is the critical question. One university installed emergency call buttons on every pillar in its underground garage. (Photos: Sandra Colangelo)

climate of fear, while a vibrant and beautiful environment is a sign of civility and engenders confidence and caring for both people and property.

Overall Design: What to Look For

(Check the items that apply to each site or situation.)

IMPORTANCE OF QUALITY AND BEAUTY

☐ Is the environment one that people can enjoy?

Security is not inimical to aesthetic value; making a place more human encourages people to use it. An inviting environment creates an image that attracts people, while a barren or sterile environment can repel potential users.

LEGIBILITY

☐ Is the design legible? Are the entrances and exits, the places to find people, and the places to find services such as washrooms or phones obvious to a pedestrian visiting a place for the first time?

The more complex a space, the more signage and other measures to increase legibility need to be considered.

AVOIDING AMBIGUITY

☐ Does the design of a space make clear the purpose of the space? Are unused and unusable "dead spaces" avoided?

NOTES

1. F. Stoks, personal communication, 1990.

2. K. Painter, *Lighting and Crime Prevention: The Edmonton Project* (Middlesex Polytechnic, U.K., 1988).

3. City of Toronto, *The Safe City: Municipal Strategies for Preventing Public Violence Against Women* (Toronto: City of Toronto Safe City Committee, 1988).

4. M. Vogel, *Design for Saint Paul Public Safety: A Guide for Making a Safer Public Realm* (City of Saint Paul: Department of Planning and Economic Development, 1993).

4

Unsafe Places: Improving or Avoiding Them

The purpose of this chapter is to discuss ways to improve places that are commonly considered unsafe. It applies the principles presented in Chapter 3 to specific conditions.

Community meetings and empirical studies have identified six types of places for priority attention in improving safety in the urban environment:

1. **Transportation-linked.** Spaces where urban residents feel vulnerable include parking structures, underground garages, and parking lots; bus stops, subways, rapid transit stations, and the route to and from the bus stop; bicycle routes and pedestrian under- and overpasses.
2. **Commercial areas** When downtown streets are empty of life at nights or on weekends, they are avoided, with disastrous social and economic consequences for cities. Commercial streets in neighborhoods and shopping malls also need special attention to ensure that users feel safe.
3. **Industrial areas** In older parts of cities and new suburban industrial parks make little provision in their design for the personal safety of workers or clients.
4. **Parks.** Often seen as unsafe places, rather than as urban amenities both in neighborhoods and in the larger regional context.
5. **Residential areas.** A basic requisite of a safe city is the ability to feel safe around one's home and in the surrounding neighborhood. This requires attention to residential streets and the design and management of housing environments.
6. **University and college campuses.** Increasingly concerned about security. Open access to facilities and extended hours are magnets that attract people to campus spaces. Large peripheral parking lots, pathways, lounges, meeting rooms, and open dorms can become unsafe places.

TRANSPORTATION-LINKED SPACES

Most people use some form of transportation, either cars, public transport, or bicycles. Yet the necessary activities of daily life, getting to and from work or school, doing shopping, seeing friends and relatives can be a dangerous activity. Poor people have to take public transport—the most unsafe option. Transit captives, users who must use public transit because they have no other options, are the most fearful and the most vulnerable. In most cities, transit captives are predominantly the poor, the elderly, women, children, and the physically handicapped. People who use public transportation feel under the most stress. Using public transport involves being in a public space, over which you have no control, with a wide range of strangers. Bus users are required to wait for periods of time on the street, where they are vulnerable to street crime. Serial rapists have followed women from public transit stops, especially if there is an isolated "entrapment spot" nearby. Subway and rapid transit users report feeling trapped and isolated in stations and in subway cars.

Cars are the transportation mode of choice in North American cities. In low-density suburban areas, automobiles are the only viable way of getting around and they provide the only access to jobs in suburban office and industrial parks. Most importantly, cars create a bubble of personal security for urban and suburban residents. Women often drive or take taxis for security reasons, especially at night. Middle class teenage girls learn to drive because this gives them a feeling of added security. Yet up to a quarter of acquaintance sexual assaults take place in this "bubble of security" which is the perfect entrapment spot.

With the increase in personal violence in urban areas, driving a car is no longer a guarantee of security as new forms of violence emerge. There is an increase in assaults and abductions in suburban mall parking lots, anonymous areas where thousands of strangers come and go. Carjackings, auto thefts with violence leading to injury or death, are on the increase and were made a federal felony in the United States in October 1993. Deliberate car accidents to lure burglary victims out of their cars is a new phenomenon in tourist cities such as Miami. Car drivers feel far less safe today than they used to and new technologies such as cellular car telephones are heavily advertised as personal security features.

Pedestrians and cars meet in underpasses and overpasses and these areas contribute to fears for personal safety. In designing under- and overpasses, traffic engineers have traditionally been concerned about ensuring traffic safety and speeding traffic flow. Now urban residents are questioning the value of pedestrian tunnels, overpasses, and skywalks because they create isolated spaces that are potential entrapment spots. In Britain and the Netherlands, citizen concerns about pedestrian safety in these spaces have resulted in new policies to drastically curtail the development of new underpasses and overpasses and to provide crossings at grade wherever possible.

Bicycle routes are newly popular as a sustainable and inexpensive way to get around urban areas. But planning for bicycle routes also needs to pay attention to security issues to ensure that routes are provided in areas with sufficient surveillance and activities, good lighting, and an adequate number of exit points.

Public Transportation on Surface Transit, Subways,
and Commuter Rail: The Problem

Personal security on public transportation systems has a major effect on ridership patterns and the financial viability of public transit. But fear of crime on public transport also affects urban dwellers' general perception of quality of life in the city and their access to jobs and services. Spending cutbacks throughout the 1980s often resulted in a reduction of safety on public transport as stations and vehicles were destaffed or maintenance and renovations were deferred. Such cutbacks have created a vicious spiral. As patrons became more anxious about their personal security, those with other options used public transport less or not at all.

Women users of public transit are particularly sensitive to security concerns. Employed women are two and three times more likely to use public transportation than employed men who are more likely to drive to work.[1] Studies in London, England, have found that women consider buses the safest way to get about compared with other modes of public transport, especially after dark. Smaller community buses are preferred because passengers are closest to the driver. Women feel less safe on rail modes, even during the day. Cars and taxis are considered the safest way to get around the city, but since women's incomes are lower than men's, women as a group are more likely to take public transport, despite their preferences and greater fear for their personal safety. [2]

Declines in ridership as a consequence of customers' concerns about personal security have been documented on the New York City transit system; in London, England; and in Toronto, Canada. In an effort to hold on to ridership, public transport agencies in these cities have given passenger security top priority

The Metropolitan Transportation Authority (MTA) in New York City has conducted extensive surveys of personal security and transit patrons' fear of crime. They conclude that concerns about personal security are a major barrier to increasing the frequency of ridership. This is particularly the case for women and older people. Women are more sensitive than men to overall environmental conditions. The MTA studies found that cleanliness and crowding are more important issues for women than men. Women also tend to feel significantly more vulnerable than men in the subway, which is an important reason why women are more likely than men to ride the local or express bus.[3] Subway users are also concerned about fare beaters, panhandlers, and the homeless in subway stations; 45 percent say that sexual harassment of women is a problem. The overriding psychological emotion when patrons enter a New York City subway station is "fear for my safety." Crime is mentioned as one of the top three subway problems by 75 percent of New York City subway users and 97 percent of patrons take precautionary measures.[4]

These findings have prompted the MTA to make changes in the quality of the subway environment to try to change users' perceptions of crime on the system. Steps taken to reduce the perception of incivilities in the environment include adding new and clean cars, removing graffiti, and restoring and cleaning stations. This contributes to users' perception of personal security. The solutions are a combination of safer design; management that gives priority to security; increasing usage, especially at off-peak hours;[5] and the active participation of users in identifying problems and solutions.

In Toronto, the Toronto Transit Commission has invited eight women's organizations to form a Women's Security Advisory Committee to advise on the design of new subway stations on two new lines. Involving women users at the initial design changes is one way to avoid costly retrofits later on.

In American and British cities, the trend to privatizing and decentralizing urban public transport systems may have unanticipated consequences for security. In British cities, large centralized systems have been sold off to small private operators. There is no centralized coordination of security nor are there personal security standards to which private operators must adhere. Solutions are left to the competition of the marketplace. This may result in safer public transport where there is real competition but this is not the case in all communities.

Surface Transit: What to Look For

(Check the items that apply to each site.)

LIGHTING

☐ Is the area adjacent to transit stops well lit so that passersby and passing automobiles can discern faces of people waiting?

☐ If there is a shelter, does it avoid overlighting so that the user does not feel like a fish in a bowl?

SIGHTLINES

☐ Are persons at transit stops clearly visible from streets or adjacent buildings?

☐ Can walls, berms, bushes, hills, or solid fences that block the view be eliminated?

☐ If there is a bus shelter, is it transparent with no obstructing advertisements or graffiti?

ADJACENT LAND USES

☐ Do adjacent land uses contribute to the lack of safety at bus stops? i.e., bars, sites of drug dealing?

Moving a bus stop several blocks may be a short-term solution. Cooperation among transit operators, planning staff, and owners might seek longer-term solutions.

Figure 4-1. A bus shelter on Broadway, Upper West Side, New York City. Note the openness of the shelter, the route map and timetable, and a sign at the top of the shelter identifying it by number and providing a telephone number to call if the shelter is vandalized. (Photo: Gerda Wekerle)

Figure 4-2. This problem bus stop is isolated from view by shops and close to an alley with potential entrapment spots. Area residents say that they avoid waiting here. (Photo: Vincenzo Pietropaolo)

AVOIDANCE OF ENTRAPMENT SPOTS

☐ If there are nearby entrapment spots created by landscaping or the built form, can they be eliminated?

☐ Is the shelter designed to reduce the possibility of entrapment through multiple exits?

MAINTENANCE

☐ Is the shelter and bus stop well maintained and free of rubbish?

☐ Is it identified by number and is a number posted to call for maintenance?

REDUCING ISOLATION

☐ If the bus stop is adjacent to vacant land, alleys, ravines, parking lots, or buildings set back far from the street, can it be moved?

Bus stops in isolated locations with poor sightlines should be moved to a spot where informal surveillance can take place, such as near a convenience store. Public telephones should be located adjacent to isolated bus stops. These locations should be part of regular police patrols.

SIGNAGE

☐ Are there passenger informational signs giving routes and times?

Long waits can be avoided and vulnerability decreased at a stop by knowing when a vehicle will arrive. Bus stops could also have vicinity maps, bus schedules, and the location of the nearest telephone. To reduce long waits, especially at night, the Toronto Transit Commission provides a phone number for each bus stop. Passengers can call ahead to a central switchboard to determine when the bus will arrive at that particular stop.

OFFENSIVE TRANSIT ADS

☐ Are there guidelines to evaluate transit ads that are violent or sexist on bus shelters, buses, and subway cars?

In Philadelphia, a women's group challenged the display of ads for *Penthouse* magazine on bus shelters on the grounds that women have a right to use public transit without fear. In Metropolitan Toronto, the company with exclusive rights to display ads in Metro bus shelters refused to display a lingerie ad of a scantily clad woman on the grounds that this was offensive to women transit users.

FORMAL SURVEILLANCE

☐ Are transit drivers able to summon emergency assistance through two-way radios?
☐ Are drivers trained to respond to emergencies?

Issuing cellular telephones or radios to bus drivers makes them a greater asset for providing eyes on the street since they are able to report on security issues along their route. This also increases the safety of both passengers and drivers.

Figure 4-3. Bus drivers can serve as informal street watchdogs. This Toronto bus driver is linked by telephone to headquarters and can call in if there are security problems. Training for drivers on how to be alert to dangerous situations on the street is essential. (Photo: Toronto Transit Commission)

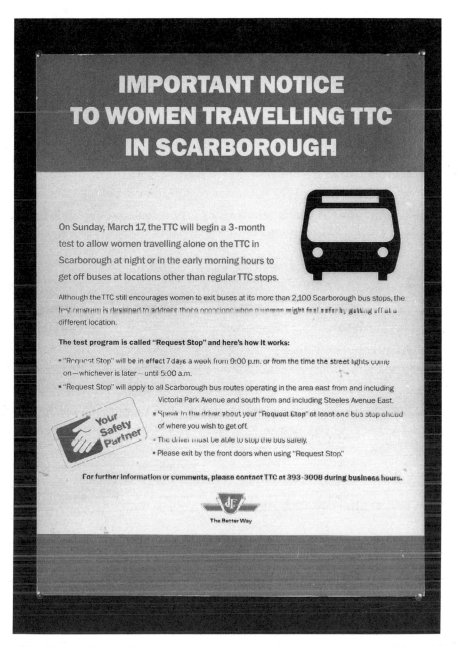

Figure 4-4. The Toronto Transit Commision initiated a Request Stop Program in 1991 in response to the dangers posed by a serial rapist who followed women home from the bus in a suburban community. After a three-month trial, the Request Stop Program was extended to the entire metropolitan area. Staten Island, New York, started a similar program in 1993. (Photo: Toronto Transit Commission)

DEMAND STOPS

☐ Is it possible to institute demand stops in evening hours, especially in high-risk areas or in suburban low-density neighborhoods?

The Toronto Transit Commission initially started a Request-Stop program in a suburban city so that after 8 P.M. women could ask the bus driver to let them off anywhere along the route, not just at designated stops. Because women passengers were dropped off closer to home, this minimized their walk from bus to home and made it more difficult for potential stalkers to follow them. After a trial, the Request-Stop program was extended to the entire Toronto Metropolitan area. Staten Island, New York, has started a Pilot Request-Stop Program.

PATROLS

☐ Does the local police force know the location of transit stops that are problems, i.e., stops where there has been a rash of robberies?

☐ Are such transit stops part of the route for community policing?

☐ Is it possible to involve persons who live or work near a dangerous bus stop—local residents, merchants, a school—to report suspicious persons as part of a Neighborhood Watch Program?

SCHEDULING AND NIGHT ROUTES

☐ Are buses scheduled to coincide with times when shifts of major employers let out, especially late at night?

☐ Can the transit authority establish a system of "night routes," routes where service is maintained for 24 hours to accommodate shift workers, office cleaners, or university students?

Scheduling decisions should give weight to public safety concerns especially since they have an unequal impact on heavy transit users: women, lower-income people, and racial and ethnic minorities.

Rapid Transit, Subways and Commuter Rail: What to Look For

(Check the items that apply to each site.)

LIGHTING

☐ Are entrances, stairwells, tunnels, and platforms well lit?

☐ Are burned-out lights replaced within a day?

☐ In commuter parking lots for transit users, is lighting adequate to see whether someone is hiding in the back of the car?

☐ Are there regular and frequent maintenance checks to replace burned out lights?

SIGHTLINES

☐ Are stations designed so that ticket takers have unobstructed sightlines of stations or platforms?

☐ Are video cameras used to observe unstaffed entrances, tunnels, and platforms?

☐ Are entrance stairways designed to eliminate hidden corners and provide a line of sight to the ticket-sellers booth?

☐ Are there mirrors at blind corners in stairwells and corridors?

☐ Can staff lunchrooms be located to increase passive surveillance of stations?

☐ Are stations concealed from main streets?

Figure 4-5. Subway ticket sellers in the Toronto subway system monitor video cameras on the platform. (Photo: Toronto Transit Commission)

Figure 4-6. Poor sightlines in this unattended underground entrance to a Toronto Light Rail Transit station. A convex mirror and possibly a video monitor could be installed. (Photo: Vincenzo Pietropaolo)

In rapid transit stations, sightlines can often be improved by eliminating alcoves or by moving kiosks. Concessions for vendors adjacent to platforms may be one solution to maintaining a continuous presence. Telephones and concessions should be grouped rather than dispersed to maintain open sightlines between token booths, entries, and activity nodes.

DESIGNATED WAITING AREAS

☐ In redesigning subway stations, is it possible to create off-hours or designated waiting areas where there is enhanced lighting, greater passenger visibility, and additional safety features?

Designated waiting areas are used by the New York City subway system to indicate to passengers during off-hours the place on the platform where they are in view of ticket takers. This also serves to concentrate passengers in certain cars rather than spreading them thinly throughout the train. In 1991, the Toronto Transit Commission installed designated waiting areas (DWAs) on all subway platforms. These areas are boldly signed, brightly lit, surveilled by video cameras, and there is an on-platform emergency button and intercom linked to transit security. The DWAs are also located so that the subway car with an attendant stops in front of the area. This contributes to passenger safety. A survey showed that 70 percent of riders say they are likely to use DWAs and women riders rated their personal safety on the subway system significantly higher after the DWAs were installed.

ENTRAPMENT SPOTS

☐ In large stations, are there alcoves or pillars that might be eliminated?

☐ Are public washrooms regularly patrolled? Could they be located near a staffed entrance?

Figure 4-7. The Toronto Transit Commission has conducted safety audits in all its subway stations. One result is the creation of Designated Waiting Areas (DWAs), surveyed via closed-circuit camera by ticket collectors. The DWAs are also equipped with emergency buttons with a voice link to security, enhanced lighting, and the train with the attendant stops in front of it. (Photo: Toronto Transit Commission)

MAINTENANCE

☐ Are subway stations, platforms, and cars maintained to eliminate the accumulation of trash and debris and to give passengers the sense that the place is cared for?

☐ Is graffiti removed within 24 hours?

☐ Are stations humanized with art or public installations related to the history of the adjacent community?

If graffiti and vandalism are left for long periods of time, this signals passengers that other antisocial behavior may go unchallenged or unseen. In Australia, the Victorian Transit Authority worked in conjunction with local groups to remove graffiti and plant community gardens in suburban rail stations. To beautify stations, the MTA in New York City has also worked with community groups adjacent to stations to create artwork reflecting local history and culture.

REDUCING ISOLATION

☐ Can little used-exits be closed at off-hours and clearly signed as closed?

☐ Have alternatives to tunnels and overpasses been considered?

☐ Are walkways to commuter parking lots located in areas with high pedestrian traffic and are they well lit?

☐ Are there emergency buttons or intercoms in tunnels, on platforms, and in each subway train?

☐ On two-level commuter trains, are there emergency buttons on each level?

☐ Are street entertainers allowed to perform in stations to maintain an ongoing activity?

☐ Are taxis available outside all stations at night?

Rapid transit station exits to isolated areas can be closed after peak hours or permanently closed. Isolated walkways or tunnels should be avoided as pathways to transit stations or bus stops. A transit authority can control street entertainers by licensing them to perform in certain stations.

FORMAL SURVEILLANCE

☐ Are all stations staffed, especially at night?

☐ Are isolated areas or areas of low traffic surveilled by video camera?

☐ Are both transit police and city police in evidence on the system?

☐ Are police assigned to specific stations?

In London's Underground, a system of community policing, "Home Beat," makes each British Transport officer responsible for a small number of stations. There is also a toll-free telephone CRIMELINE to report crime on the underground.

SIGNAGE

☐ Is signage in rapid transit stations clear so that passengers can find exits and platforms quickly with a minimum of wandering around?

☐ Are maps of the subway system and transfer points distributed so that every subway user can see them?

Figure 4-8. In focus groups on women's transit safety, women told the Toronto Transit Commission (TTC) that they did not feel free to press the emergency strip in each subway car if they were being threatened or sexually harassed. The TTC conducted an educational campaign encouraging women to use the strips in case of harassment or fear of assault. (Photo: Toronto Transit Commission)

Figure 4-9. All Paris Metro station platforms have these alarm boxes. The top third is used to call the station manager in case of danger or emergency, the middle cuts the power to the rail if someone falls on the tracks, the bottom segment holds a fire extinguisher. (Photo: Gerda Wekerle)

Signage in subway stations can be confusing, incomplete, or inconsistent. Often there are limited maps. One solution is to color code floor paths to connecting trains.

PUBLIC EDUCATION

☐ Do transit posters inform passengers of the security features of the system?

Making passengers aware of the transit security program is one way to reduce fear of crime and to encourage people to use rapid transit systems more. The Toronto Transit system has developed a series of posters to increase passengers' awareness of safety features. Public education displays at key locations stress crime prevention. In Australia, the Victorian Transit Authority has started a TravelSafe Program which is widely advertised.

ENFORCING THE RULES

☐ Does the signage make clear the expectations of behavior on the transit system? e.g., no littering or indecent language.

☐ Is there a program in place to apprehend fare skippers?

Figure 4-10   This transit map in the Paris Metro orients commuters to the vicinity of the station that they are exiting. (Photo: Gerda Wekerle)

Figure 4-11. In Melbourne, Australia, transit authorities recognize the link between uncivil behavior and fear of crime. (Photo: Carolyn Whitzman)

In New York City, transit police were able to reduce overall crime rates on the subway system by vigorous efforts to arrest and charge fare evaders. One in seven fare evaders caught had outstanding warrants for more serious crimes.

MANAGEMENT

☐   Is there a station manager in charge of each station with a name and address listed for patrons to contact in case of complaints?

Figure 4-12. Making subway stations more attractive through public art and natural lighting makes transit users feel less fearful. (Photo: Toronto Transit Commission)

☐ Does the transit authority have programs in place to train frontline staff in how to respond to sexual assaults and other incidents of personal violence?

New York City has a station manager program. The visibility of management, information, and maintenance work together in making areas secure and increase patrons' perception of personal security. The Toronto Transit Commission has put in place a program developed by the Equal Opportunity Program that trains staff in how to respond to sexual assault cases. Frontline workers are given tear-off cards with phone numbers of rape crisis lines and women's shelters.

CONSULTATION

☐ In the development and redevelopment of rapid transit stations, is security staff consulted and involved in evaluating plans and retrofits?

☐ Are user groups that are heavy transit users—minority groups, the elderly, women, and schoolchildren—consulted on a regular basis concerning their sense of security and fear of crime on the transit system?

☐ Is there a security advisory committee of citizens to involve transit users in an ongoing way in defining issues and solutions to public safety on the transit system?

The Toronto Transit Commission has initiated several approaches to citizen involvement. Focus group meetings with representatives of women's groups highlighted women's fear of crime on the transit system. Participatory research projects conducted jointly with community women's groups and Metro Police evaluated the design of subway stations and transit stops and made recommendations to improve safety, which have been implemented. A safety education program is delivered to schools and other groups and a film on women's safety, jointly funded by the transit agency, was shown on prime time television.

TRANSIT ALTERNATIVES

☐ In low-density suburban areas, is it possible to set up alternative transit options to conventional buses, e.g., community buses or subsidized taxis, which provide more frequent service?

Figure 4-13. A community bus links a shopping mall with nearby suburban residential areas and a seniors' complex in Toronto. By reducing waiting times on suburban streets, the community bus contributes to urban safety. (Photo: Gerda Wekerle)

☐ At the end of suburban bus lines, are taxi services available, and are they coordinated with the bus service?

☐ Does the transit authority encourage specialized van services by employers, seniors' centers, or women's groups to provide para-transit for these underserved groups?

☐ If para-transit is provided for the physically handicapped, has attention been paid to personal safety concerns in the location of waiting and drop-off areas?

☐ On para-transit systems for the physically handicapped, is there a system in place to monitor drivers to prevent sexual harassment of passengers?

The low density and design of suburban areas, with few through streets and many cul-de-sacs, makes service with regular buses uneconomical. Suburban residents with limited or no access to private automobiles are put at risk when they must walk long distances to the nearest bus stop to wait for a bus that comes infrequently. Community-based alternatives to regular buses increase safety in low-density suburban areas.

Since 1982, British local authorities have funded Women's Safe Transport schemes—minibuses that run at night and provide door-to-door service for women within a local area. These are funded either by national Safer Cities funds, by community development grants, or by funding from municipal women's committees within local government.

Women who are physically handicapped are at far greater risk for sexual harassment and sexual assault. Para-transit for physically handicapped passengers is frequently provided by private contractors. Transit authorities have a responsibility to ensure the safety and well-being of passengers who are the most vulnerable.

Cars—Parking Garages and Parking Lots: The Problem

Underground parking garages are one of the most problematic kinds of urban space, according to studies in Toronto, Manchester, London, and Amsterdam. Combining a single use—car storage—with relative isolation, noise, and visual barriers leads to underground garages being perceived as prime spots for sexual assault and muggings. In addition, many garages are poorly designed and maintained. In some commercial buildings, a security corral with enhanced security provided by video cameras and car jockeys is a perk made available to top executives. Such two-tier security arrangements only serve to underscore the public's perception that security is a problem in underground garages.

Some cities have drafted bylaws to address personal security in parking structures. In the City of Toronto, an amendment to the housing bylaw regarding security in residential underground parking garages was adopted in 1988, and a proposed amendment to the building code should eventually cover all underground parking garages and multistory car parking facilities, including mixed residential-commercial and commercial garages. Minneapolis passed a bylaw governing safety and design criteria in parking garages in 1989. But bylaws are only the beginning of the potential security measures that can be taken. In Frankfurt, Germany, parking garages on lands leased from the city are required to provide women-only parking spaces in secure locations near an attendant or exit. A number of workplaces offer underground garage escort services to employees working late.

While underground parking garages have received attention, security issues relating to surface parking lots have been neglected. Like underground garages, surface lots can be badly designed, poorly lit, and isolated. Surface parking lots range from small three- or four-space lots behind, in front of, or adjacent to buildings, to very large lots with thousands of spaces found around shopping malls. Where lots are larger than 50 car spaces, additional precautions are necessary.

Underground and Multi-Story Parking Garages: What to Look For

(Check the items that apply to each site.)

LIGHTING

☐ Is the garage lit to the minimum standard of an average of five footcandles?

☐ Are light fixtures protected from breakage by some means such as wired glass?

☐ Is the light consistent?

☐ Are exit corridors lit to five footcandles in corridors?

☐ Is the lighting level ten footcandles in stairways?

☐ Are the walls and ceilings painted white or another light color?

A commonsense way to measure the level and consistency of lighting is: "Can you see a person hiding in the backseat of your car before entering?" Whitewashing walls not only increases the efficiency of the light, it also looks cleaner and more pleasant than bare concrete.

SIGHTLINES

☐ Are stairwells and elevators located where they can be viewed by the maximum number of people?

☐ Are stairwells glass enclosed and located on an exterior wall?

☐ Is the major route(s) from the garage to the exit(s) free of sharp turns?

☐ If there are sharp turns or pillars obstructing sightlines, can sightlines be improved by using mirrors or other methods?

Figure 4-14. This residential parking garage violates all the rules. It is wide open, the lock is broken, lighting is inadequate, and concrete walls absorb the light. (Photo: Carolyn Whitzman)

Figure 4-15. The City Hall parking garage complex in Toronto offers good lighting (improved by painting walls and ceiling white) and relatively clear sightlines. Missing are good directional signs and any indication of how to summon help. (Photo: Vincenzo Pietropaolo)

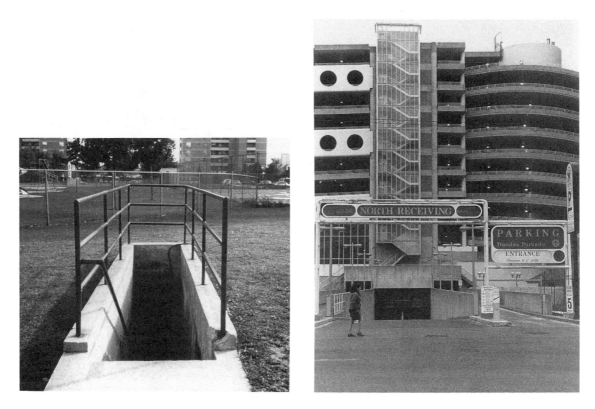

Figure 4-16. The entrance/exit to this suburban apartment garage is dark and enclosed, with no signage and limited sightlines. (Photo: Gerda Wekerle)

Figure 4-17. A glassed-in staircase at this commercial garage in Toronto's Eaton Center in the downtown area increases visibility and surveillance by passersby. (Photo: Sandra Colangelo)

ENTRAPMENT SPOTS

☐ Do doors have windows so people can see into an elevator lobby or into the area between fire doors?

☐ Is the interior of elevator cabs visible from the exterior?

☐ Are any hiding places illuminated or closed off?

☐ Are potential entrapment areas, such as storerooms, kept locked?

ATTENDANTS

☐ Are attendants' booths located so that there are good sightlines?

☐ Are attendants trained to respond to emergencies?

Some commercial garages have car jockeys who park cars and provide a continuous presence on all parking levels.

MAINTENANCE

☐ Are burned-out light bulbs and vandalism repaired promptly?

☐ Are there numbers posted to report maintenance problems?

☐ Are locking devices in residential garages in good repair to keep nonresidents out?

Figure 4-18. A staffed entrance to a parking garage provides information on how to get to different destinations as well as added security. (Photo: Sandra Colangelo)

FORMAL SURVEILLANCE THROUGH PATROLS

☐ Is there some form of formal surveillance, such as regular patrols by maintenance staff, security personnel, or by pairs of residents in residential garages?

☐ Is the individual making an inspection readily identified?

☐ Are they trained to respond to emergencies?

FORMAL SURVEILLANCE THROUGH HARDWARE

☐ In larger commercial garages, are there emergency telephones on each level with the accompanying raised illuminated international telephone signs?

☐ Are there emergency buttons, a sound-activated alarm, or a telephone on each floor?

☐ Are these emergency systems centrally located and clearly signed?

☐ Are there video cameras in stairwells, elevators, lobbies, at vehicle entrances and exits?

☐ Is all audio and visual equipment monitored during facility operating hours?

☐ Are the people who monitor audio or video emergency systems trained in using the equipment and to respond to emergencies?

☐ Are they responsible for monitoring a reasonable number of cameras and are personnel regularly evaluated?

SIGNAGE

☐ Do signs direct garage users to stairs, elevators, escalators, or exits?

Figure 4-19. Signs like this one in parking garages put users on the alert. (Photo: Sandra Colangelo)

☐ Are there directional signs to offices, fire extinguishers, and emergency buttons?

☐ At the point of exit, is there information describing the location level or zone of a parked car via numbers, letters, or color coding?

☐ Can users orient themselves to aboveground streets or buildings to find the closest exit?

☐ Are standard international symbols used for fire extinguishers and emergency alarms?

☐ Are there signs at entrances clearly advising customers of the type of security system provided on premises?

☐ Are there signs telling patrons to lock their cars and be alert?

DESIGNATED SPACES OR ESCORTS

☐ In office building garages, is it possible to reserve certain spots near the attendant for people who regularly work late, especially female office workers?

☐ Are designated spots for people with disabilities near an attendant, if there is one, or otherwise near a safe exit?

☐ Can an escort service be provided in large workplaces by the building owner or the workplace?

☐ Is there a sign at the entrance clearly defining the escort service and hours available?

In Frankfurt, Germany, parking garages on city-owned land provide women-only parking

Figure 4-20. Finding your car is difficult in many parking garages when every floor looks the same. In this Halifax hotel parking garage, the pink elephants make it easy to remember the floor your car is on. The white ceilings and walls reflect light to brighten the garage. (Photo: Gerda Wekerle)

spaces near an attendant or a major circulation path. Women-only parking spaces have spread to other German cities. The City of Toronto Parking Authority is developing an escort service after 8 P.M. for garage users in the large commercial City Hall Parking Garage. This will benefit both civic staff and the public.

ALL-NIGHT CAR PARKS

☐ For 24-hour multistory car parks, is there an attendant on duty at all times who is trained to respond to emergencies?

Surface Parking Lots: What to Look For

(Check the items that apply to each site).

LIGHTING

☐ Is lighting adequate to see the inside of a car's backseat before entering the car?

☐ Is lighting consistent, avoiding shadows?

☐ Is there a regular maintenance program to replace burned-out lights?

SIGHTLINES

☐ Do parking lot users have clear sightlines from the entrance through the lot?

Figure 4-21. Energy conservation measures and increasing security through better lighting are in conflict at this college campus parking lot. (Photo: David Orsini)

Figure 4-22. This parking lot behind the Broadcast Center in Regina, Saskatchewan, is considered "scary" by workers. It is isolated behind the building with long blank walls with niches built into them. It faces another parking lot and there is a long walk to the front entrance of the building. (Photo: Gerda Wekerle)

☐ Are sightlines within and to the lots maximized through the elimination of dense bushes or tree landscaping?

☐ Do solid fences or advertisements block the view?

☐ Can unnecessary buildings or sheds be moved?

☐ Can parking lots be divided into smaller segments?

Designers frequently aim to screen surface lots from public view through the use of berms, landscaping, or fencing. Adding trees and landscaping to parking lots is a new trend. Trees with high canopies or low landscaping that is regularly pruned would maintain sightlines. In entryways off commercial streets, wrought iron fencing or low-growth, low maintenance bushes are preferable to other barriers. Some bushes require a high level of maintenance in order to avoid growing too high for adequate sightlines or developing gaps that could be used as a hiding spot.

ATTENDANTS

☐ Is there a single entry/exit to allow supervision of vehicles by an attendant?

☐ Are attendants trained to know how to respond in an emergency?

☐ Are they periodically supervised and audited?

AVOIDING ENTRAPMENT

☐ If there is no attendant, are there several well-lit, clearly marked entrances in order to prevent the lot from acting as an entrapment spot?

☐ Is the parking lot at the side or back of the building adjacent to alcoves or waste spaces?

Parking lots in front of convenience stores should be discouraged. While marginally safer and more convenient for the car user, these parking lots weaken the link between building and street, and are a traffic safety hazard as well.

INFORMAL SURVEILLANCE

- ☐ Is informal surveillance of surface lots or parking for residences encouraged through placement of windows in new buildings so that they overlook the lot?
- ☐ Can shopping malls be redesigned to have windows overlooking parking lots?
- ☐ Can retail kiosks be added to the edge of a parking lot?

In housing developments, residents prefer parking that is attached to individual units and that can be observed from the unit, to corral parking that is at a distance from the housing unit.

FORMAL SURVEILLANCE AND HARDWARE

- ☐ In larger lots, are there regular patrols by trained staff?
- ☐ Are there emergency telephones throughout the lots with accompanying raised, illuminated international telephone signs?
- ☐ Is there some other way to summon help promptly?

Universities with large surface parking lots have pioneered using emergency telephones linked directly to university security offices. Commercial operators have been slow to follow suit, although massive surface lots surrounding suburban shopping malls could benefit from this security feature.

Figure 4-23. A vast commuter parking lot for subway users is isolated behind the station and cut off by expressway ramps. Attendants collect money in the morning when commuters park their cars, but at night there are no attendants and pools of darkness are created by the many burned-out lights in the lot. (Photo: Gerda Wekerle)

Figure 4-24. The upper level of this parking structure is overlooked by stores and an entrance to several movie theaters. Movie patrons provide a steady stream of pedestrian traffic. (Photo: Gerda Wekerle)

SIGNAGE

☐ Are there location identification signs in larger lots so that passengers can more easily locate their cars?

DESIGNATED SPACES OR ESCORTS

☐ In office building lots, is there provision for an escort service or for reserved spots close to the building entrance for people who regularly work late?

☐ Are priority parking spots for people with disabilities located near the parking attendant when there is one, and near an exit to the street or an accessible elevator when there is no attendant?

When Pedestrians and Cars Meet—Under- and Overpasses:
The Problem

Grade separation occurs when tunnels or overpasses separate pedestrian or car traffic. While the rationale for building tunnels or overpasses varies (ranging from traffic safety, to deconcentrating pedestrian traffic, to concentrating the opportunities for commercial profit), the net result is that opportunities for natural surveillance are diminished.

Pedestrian underpasses create security problems, especially when there are dangerous places in the immediate vicinity. The cities of Manchester, Wandsworth, Glasgow, Sheffield, Portsmouth, and Poole in the United Kingdom, and several cities in the Netherlands, have a policy to construct no more pedestrian underpasses and to replace existing underpasses, where possible, by improved ground level facilities.

Traffic safety can be realized by means other than pedestrian underpasses. These include: level crossings at railroads, greater use of pedestrian crossings, widening the sidewalk where pedestrian traffic is great, and limiting car traffic through bus and bicycle lanes.

Underground pedestrian malls present some of the same problems as tunnels. They drain life from downtown streets. While informal surveillance in underground malls is possible during hours in which stores are open, they can be very scary places after hours. The question of formal surveillance or policing is also difficult to resolve in private malls. There have been concerns expressed about overzealousness on the part of private security firms, who in some cases are accused of racial or income discrimination when they force youths or homeless people to vacate the premises.

Existing underground pedestrian pathways, especially those malls in the center city found under office buildings, can't be wished away. In the case of existing malls, the provision of alternate aboveground routes, a good way-finding system, and the introduction of design standards for retrofitting existing pathways, as well as new pathways, are all priorities.

Pedestrian Tunnels and Underpasses: What to Look For

(Check the items that apply to each site.)

AVOIDANCE OF THE NECESSITY FOR GRADE SEPARATION

☐ Is this tunnel, underpass, or overpass necessary, i.e., are there no alternatives?

☐ If there are overriding reasons why a tunnel should continue to exist, are there signs at each end of the tunnel indicating where the tunnel leads?

☐ Is there an alternative route to using the tunnel during off-hours?

Northern cities like Montreal and Toronto built downtown pedestrian systems in the 1960s as a solution to the cold weather. Experience since then has shown that pedestrian tunnel systems suck activity off the streets and keep it underground. The extension of downtown pedestrian tunnel networks is still under debate in Toronto and elsewhere. The develop

Figure 4-25. Safety from cars or muggers? That was the choice planners had to make at this pedestrian underpass in Amsterdam which was built to protect pedestrians from cars at an intersection where five arterial roads meet. The underpass was closed off after pedestrians using it were threatened. The street crossings for pedestrians are still hazardous. (Photo: Gerda Wekerle)

ment of pedestrian tunnels outside the downtown area should be reviewed from a security perspective, in consultation with the community.

CLOSURE OF TUNNELS AFTER HOURS

☐ Is the tunnel leading to places that are not open 24 hours (e.g., the subway system) kept locked when these places are not open?

☐ Do signs at street level indicate the hours when a tunnel is open and an alternate route?

DIMENSIONS

☐ Are new tunnels at least 12 feet in width and ten feet in height?

This avoids the claustrophobic quality of some tunnels and allows a quick turn-around in the case of emergency.

LIGHTING

☐ Is the tunnel lit from natural or artificial sources to a standard of no less than four footcandles?

☐ Is the lighting fixture protected by wired glass or some other method?

☐ Is the lighting regularly checked and is there a number posted so that users can report maintenance problems?

Figure 4-26. Techworld Plaza in Washington, D.C., with its food kiosks and boutiques, is full of local office workers and tourists staying at nearby hotels during the day. The sign alerts people that the underground mall is closed after 6 P.M, Sundays, and holidays. Closing the mall ensures that unsuspecting tourists or shoppers are not trapped in an underground system at times when there is very little pedestrian traffic. (Photo: Gerda Wekerle)

Figure 4-27. Recent improvements to this underpass included better pedestrian lighting and the glassing in of the walkway to screen out mud and carbon monoxide. Exits to the street are provided at two points. The underpass is now tolerable, but still hardly pleasant, and the improvements have limited the number of escape routes available. (Photo: Vincenzo Pietropaolo)

MAINTENANCE

☐ Are the surfaces of the tunnel clean, light, easy to maintain, and reflective?

AVOIDANCE OF SHARP CORNERS

☐ Is the tunnel straight and without recesses?

☐ If it is necessary that the tunnel take a turn of more than 60 degrees, is there an angled full-length aluminum mirror placed so that pedestrians can see around the corner?

Small convex mirrors, often used in subway stairwells, are difficult to see and do not provide the desired security.

FORMAL SURVEILLANCE

☐ If the tunnel is more than 100 feet long, is there an emergency telephone or some other alarm device?

ACTIVITY GENERATORS

☐ If the tunnel is long and well used during some point in the day, are there other activity generators that can be added to make it safer at other times?

Tunnels can be equipped with pay telephones, garbage containers, washrooms, and even stores. These activity-generating elements should be placed adjacent to one another.

Figures 4-28 and 4-29. Skywalks link downtown stores and office buildings in Minneapolis, Minnesota. They create a semiprivate space that can be closed at off-hours and that sucks activities and pedestrians off the public streets. Note how different designs either decrease surveillance into the skywalk or encourage it. (Photos: Gerda Wekerle)

ENTRANCE TO TUNNEL

☐ Is the entrance and exit of a tunnel visible from stores, residences or from frequent pedestrian traffic?

SKYWALKS

☐ Are skywalks designed so that passersby at ground level can see pedestrians clearly?

☐ Are skywalk entrances closed after hours?

☐ To avoid confusion do signs clearly indicate how to get through the skywalk system?

Bicycle Routes: The Problem

In an effort to reduce traffic congestion and pollution, cities are increasingly turning to the bicycle. While bicycle commuting and a wide system of bicycle routes for recreation are a commonplace feature of many British and European cities, this is relatively new in North America. To encourage an increase in bicycle commuting, cities must develop a good safe system of through bicycle routes that connect areas of employment and outlying residential areas. Too often, bicycle routes have been planned solely for recreational use, without taking into account the needs of commuters. Planning of bicycle routes has important security implications, for not only are some routes isolated, especially at night, but often bicyclists are isolated on trails with a limited number of entrances and exits. In the Netherlands, planners and citizens have provided leadership in making bicycle routes safer.

Bicycle Routes: What to Look For

(Check the items that apply to each site.)

SYSTEM OF THROUGH ROUTES

☐ Is there a clear system of through routes on city streets, preferably not separated by visual barriers?

☐ Are the routes clearly signposted, not only on the route but along major roads feeding into the route?

☐ Are commuting routes chosen not only for convenience and lack of detours, but also for security?

This means locating bicycle routes adjacent to areas of high pedestrian and car traffic during the day and evening, with as much continuous building, as few "empty spaces," and as few underground crossings as possible. Separating bicycle paths from both pedestrian and automobile traffic makes them less safe.

RECREATIONAL ROUTES

☐ Are recreational routes designed to have at least one clearly marked "exit" to an area of high pedestrian and car traffic every 500 meters/yards?

SIGNAGE

☐ Are bicycle routes adequately signposted so that people can find them and stay on them?

☐ Do entrances to routes through isolated areas such as parks and industrial areas indicate, in words and through the use of maps, alternate night routes, as well as the fact that the route will be entering an isolated area?

LIGHTING AND SIGHTLINES

☐ Are routes well lit?

☐ Do they avoid underground crossings?

☐ Are high bushes and dense clusters of trees avoided immediately adjacent to the route?

☐ Is shrubbery trimmed at predicted stop points such as road crossings?

Bicycle parking is often designated to the leftover parts of buildings and streets. All parking, including bicycle parking, should ideally be located where it can be viewed by the individual who owns the vehicle. Failing that, informal surveillance should be possible or the bicycle parking should be provided in a secure place.

FORMAL SURVEILLANCE OF ROUTES

☐ Does the police force regularly patrol bicycle paths either by foot or bicycle patrols?

☐ Can bicycle parking spaces be informally overlooked from streets, buildings, or parking attendants?

Figure 4-30.   Amsterdam is one city where there is a network of bicycle lanes, physically but not visually separated from street and pedestrian traffic. (Photo: Gerda Wekerle)

Figure 4-31.   In the city of Avignon, France, the bicyle route is also separated from pedestrian and car traffic. (Photo: Gerda Wekerle)

Figure 4-32.   This bike route links a residential area with the center of Almere, a suburban community in the Netherlands. Bicyclists have complained that the separation from cars and pedestrians makes them feel less safe. (Photo: Carolyn Whitzman)

Figure 4-33. Bicycle parking at the front of a building, overlooked by windows and entrance, makes people feel safer when getting on or off their bike. (Photo: Carolyn Whitzman)

COMMERCIAL AREAS

Central Business District: The Problem

The concentration of business in downtown areas and the resultant loss of grade-level housing and commercial functions has been a feature of North American and European cities in the late 20th century. While very busy during the working day, Central Business Districts (CBDs) often become deserted after dark. This has security implications, not only for the hidden army of night workers, including cleaners, hospital workers, waiters, and other service staff, but for the many office and service workers who work overtime, as well as for people enjoying entertainment functions found in the Central Business District.

In many larger cities, head office or back office functions have moved out of downtown office towers and into suburban subcenters. This has contributed to high vacancy rates in downtown office buildings and in adjacent commercial strips. The result is a downtown that attracts fewer and fewer people as stores close, streets and sidewalks are uncared for, and graffiti and garbage proliferate. In some cities, attempts to halt the decline through the construction of large suburban-type shopping plazas with acres of parking lots merely contributes to the downward spiral. The mall becomes a heavily guarded enclave for shoppers with automobiles, turning its back on adjacent streets and neighborhoods and attracting any street-level activities into the interior spaces of the mall.

A planning goal is to increase the "ownership" and attraction of downtown streets, and especially to increase the number of people about at night. Good examples of municipal government and business cooperation are First Night, an alcohol-free New Year's celebration currently organized in about 20 North American cities. Downtown streets are blocked off for street theater and entertainment. Building owners open up lobbies and plazas for activities. Paris has initiated midsummer night music festivals, inviting amateur musicians to play on street corners and in plazas throughout the city. Annual street festivals and carnivals also bring people into the city center.

The city of Nottingham, England, commissioned Peat Marwick, a management consulting firm, to do a "crime audit" of the impact of fear of crime on shopping and leisure activities in the city center. The study concluded that avoidance of the city center due to fear of crime cost the city £12 million of lost business, 670 foregone job opportunities, and £84 million of lost profits.[6]

In response, Nottingham began a community safety project focusing on the city center, with particular attention to the safety of vulnerable groups, especially women and the elderly. Attention was directed to urban design that would reduce opportunities for crime through:

1. design for safe pedestrian corridors by improving lighting and replacing underpasses by surface crossings
2. considering the safety of people and property together
3. using opportunities to enhance natural surveillance
4. good maintenance to avoid images of neglect
5. taking a systemic view to avoid creating new problems
6. partnership with the private sector to improve car parks, access to public transport, and information sharing
7. establishing a city center "pub watch" to deal with drink-related offenses

In New York City, zoning incentives encourage owners of large commercial buildings to create plazas and open space that will be attractive to users by providing flexible seating, food services, and design that maximizes sunshine.[7] This has increased activities and the range of users in downtown plazas and, in some cases, has pushed out such undesirable activities as drug dealing.

Central Business District: What to Look For

(Check the items that apply to each site.)

INFORMAL SURVEILLANCE THROUGH GENERATING STREET-RELATED EVENING ACTIVITY

☐ Do commercial buildings have retail street frontages?

☐ Are commercial uses that are open late, such as restaurants and theaters, encouraged at street level?

☐ Do these retail uses have glass walls fronting main streets or are there sidewalk patios adjacent to the street?

Figure 4-34. This bleak streetscape is typical of downtown areas in many midwestern cities. At this intersection in downtown Regina, Saskatchewan, six-lane arterial roads have empty lots on two corners and hotels with blank facades on the other two corners. In the evenings and on weekends, there is little pedestrian or car traffic, and just crossing the street feels intimidating. (Photo: Gerda Wekerle)

☐ Are street vendors and street entertainers encouraged in the CBD?
☐ Do plazas provide adequate seating?
☐ Do food services or other activities attract people?

REDUCTION OF ENTRAPMENT SPOTS

☐ Are plazas and parks in the CBD at street level, rather than below or above grade?
☐ Are alleyways and loading docks well lit?
☐ Can they be fenced at night or when not in use?

LAND USE MIX — HOUSING

☐ Are there mixed-income housing units with appropriate services in the CBD?
☐ Are they of sufficient scale to generate activity and demand for local services?

TRAFFIC CALMING[8]

☐ Has the city taken measures to reduce the speed and density of traffic to make streets more pedestrian friendly?

Figure 4-35. A weekly farmer's market held on the square of Toronto's City Hall benefits both workers in the core area and downtown residents. It adds activities and brings new people into the square. Other regular activities in the square include ice skating in the winter and summer concerts. (Photo: Gerda Wekerle)

CENTRAL ACTIVITY CORRIDORS

☐ Are areas of high nighttime use grouped together to concentrate activity, e.g., a theater district and restaurants?

☐ Is this supported by public transport and parking facilities?

In Bradford, England, a safe corridor scheme links the shopping center with the entertainment and cultural area of the city and has included improvements to underpasses and lighting. In Birmingham, England, the police, local businesses, and city council have developed a closed-circuit television system for the central shopping area to reduce street crime and increase the confidence of users.[9]

MAINTENANCE

☐ Are streets, plazas, and small parks in city centers maintained and kept clean of trash to give the impression of ownership, care, and security to passersby?

PARKING

☐ Is optional on-street parking or parking in surface lots available in the evening?

☐ Are supervised women-only parking spots available in parking garages?

☐ Do large facilities provide escort services?

Figure 4-36. The most heavily used plaza in New York City, Rockefeller Center, is popular with skaters, sightseers, and shoppers. It even attracts wedding parties. The restaurant overlooks the skating rink. (Photo: Gerda Wekerle)

Figure 4-37. This outdoor restaurant in Toronto's financial district is located near theaters and brings activities on to the street. (Photo: Gerda Wekerle)

LATE-NIGHT TRANSPORT SERVICES

☐ Is late-night bus service available throughout the city center?

Metropolitan Toronto has in place a network of all-night bus and streetcar service to accommodate shift workers and people who come to the city center for entertainment. Some British Safer Cities projects have funded city center late-night bus services.

DRINKING-RELATED OFFENSES

☐ Is there a city center "bar watch" to deal with drink-related offenses?

☐ Are staff of bars trained to prevent violence-related offenses?

Downtown Commercial/Office Developments: What to Look For

(Check the items that apply to each site.)

FORMAL SURVEILLANCE

☐ Is there a central security desk and is it visible?

☐ After regular work hours, does security monitor who enters an office building?

☐ Do parking garages attached to downtown office buildings or malls provide an escort service?

☐ Do they provide designated parking spaces near an attendant or escort services for people who will be working late and who may have security concerns?

☐ Are offices connected directly to security staff?

☐ Does security staff know how to respond in emergencies?

CLUSTERING STORES THAT ARE OPEN LATE

☐ Are stores that stay open late located near the entrance of the building so that these activities will gain greater security by being clustered?

RECEPTIONIST AREA

☐ Does the receptionist have clear sightlines of the approach to his/her workstation from the door?

☐ Can the receptionist contact security staff or other workers in case of an emergency?

WASHROOM ACCESS

☐ Is washroom access limited by a key system?

Figure 4-38. Toronto's bicycle police officers patrol the downtown core and some parks. Response times are often faster with bicycles than with patrol cars in heavy downtown traffic. The bicycle police report that people are less intimidated and talk to them more when they are on bicycles. (Photo: Gerda Wekerle)

Commercial Streets in Neighborhoods: The Problem

A typical pattern is that a community's commercial area declines first, followed by the rest of the community. Declining commercial areas may be taken over by gangs and criminal elements. When large chainstores leave, they are replaced by convenience stores. Owners, employees, and customers may be driven out by crime and evidence of decline.[10]

Neighborhood commercial streets are often used in the evening and nighttime. It is on these streets that convenience stores and transit stops are most often located. Recent developments have eroded the traditional pattern of housing above shops, with its potential of informal surveillance. The social value of frequenting local businesses has declined, along with the concept of local businesspeople "watching out" on the street.

Twenty-four hour fast food and convenience outlets, with their attendant front-door parking strips, create gaps in the streetscape, and sometimes serve as hangouts for illicit activity. While hanging out on the local street corner is neither illegal nor antisocial per se, it can be perceived as frightening if only one group (e.g., teenaged boys, street people) is evident. On some main streets, drug dealing and sex trade businesses have become established, increasing residents' levels of fear. In some cities, neighborhood residents have tried to have the operating license revoked of restaurants or bars that persistently house drug dealing.[11] The goal is not to clear out the people presently using the street as a social or commercial gathering place, but to leaven the mix with a greater variety of people, which may help to curb antisocial behaviour.

Violent robberies of corner stores, especially at night, have become a fact of life in major cities.[12] Responses often involve introducing hardware, such as locked doors with buzzer systems (which may allow discrimination against minority customers), video cameras, and iron gates over windows. "Soft" design solutions, such as making sure that stores are well lit and cashiers are visible from the street in front of unencumbered windows, might be more effective and, at the same time, don't contribute to people's fear of crime. City licensing commissions could require stores that stay open late, when staff is at greatest risk, to maintain a minimum level of security. Insurance companies could offer lower rates. Mississauga, a municipality in the province of Ontario, Canada, has enacted a bylaw banning convenience stores from remaining open between midnight and 5 A.M.—and imposing fines up to $50,000 if they choose to remain open.

Commercial Streets: What to Look For

(Check the items that apply to each site.)

HOUSING ABOVE STORES

☐ Is housing available or planned above stores?

☐ Do balconies and windows of living areas in new and existing upper-story housing along commercial streets overlook the street?

SIGNAGE

☐ Are the location of telephones, toilets, and baby-changing facilities in public establishments along commercial streets clearly signed?

Telephones and well-equipped toilets attract customers during the day. Telephones and

Figure 4-39. Suburban commercial strips are oriented to cars, not pedestrians. Each franchise store has its own parking lot adjacent to the sidewalk. Parking lots become hangouts for illicit activity, including drug dealing and prostitution, in some cities. Daylight abductions of women waiting at bus stops on streets like this indicate that they are often unsafe due to the isolation of pedestrians. Cars traveling at fast speeds on arterial roads do not generally provide eyes on the street. (Photo: Gerda Wekerle)

public toilets can also be a necessity in the evening and at night. They should be located in or near a restaurant or store that has late-open hours. Store owners and local business associations may also wish to institute a "green light," "safe haven," or other security program. In one neighborhood of San Francisco, stores, restaurants, and bars that display a "safe haven" sign offer emergency phone calls or simply a safe place to escape a scary situation.

TOILETS

☐ Are public toilets located in high traffic areas rather than in isolated out-of-the way locations?

☐ Are approaches highly visible so that people cannot loiter or sneak in?

The entrances to toilets near playgrounds should be visible from the playgrounds.

☐ Is it possible to bring other activities to the toilets?

Emergency or regular telephones should be near toilets. Other activities that might encourage use at or around toilets include baby-changing tables, baby nursing stations, vending machines, and places to rest.

Figure 4-40. These portable public toilets in Paris, France, are strategically located on commercial streets or adjacent to rapid transit stations. They are locked and charge a small fee for use. They are too small to sleep in to prevent the homeless from inhabiting them. (Photo: Gerda Wekerle)

☐ Where toilets are especially necessary and especially unsafe, are there attendants?

☐ Is vandalism and graffiti regularly cleaned?

The quality of finish, maintenance, amenities, or hot water are all important to pleasant and safe-feeling toilets. Toilets are often abused because they are unhygenic. Public toilets (i.e., those in parks and community centers directly or indirectly owned by the city), and toilets used by the public (commercial establishments such as restaurants and department stores must allow customers to use their toilets), are often located in inconvenient locations, are poorly signed, and are avoided by some members of the public because of security concerns. If people are using other places to relieve themselves, this reinforces a negative image of an area. In Paris, the city has located new, clean, modernistically designed public toilets on the sidewalks of major arterial streets. These are coin operated (for a small fee). The drawback is that they are not wheelchair accessible. Design solutions should be possible to make public toilets available and accessible in safe locations.

INTENSIFICATION OF USE

☐ Are street vendors or street entertainers allowed?

☐ Is there room for sidewalk cafés and other activity intensifiers on commercial streets?

The criteria for licensing street vendors and sidewalk cafés should take into account the need to improve public safety. The goal is to get a variety of people hanging out on neighborhood commercial streets in the evening, not to exclude certain groups.

Figure 4-41. This 24-hour newsstand in New York City provides a constant set of eyes on the street and attracts pedestrian traffic. (Photo: Gerda Wekerle)

Figure 4-42. A newsstand on Paris's Champs-Elysées. The wide sidewalks, pedestrian-oriented lighting, and activities make people feel comfortable walking here. (Photo: Gerda Wekerle)

Figure 4-43. Outdoor cafés and pubs in Amsterdam attract strollers and people just watching the world go by. (Photo: Gerda Wekerle)

Figure 4-44. Bloor West Village, Toronto, a neighborhood-based commercial shopping strip on a Saturday morning. Besides food stores, there are also ethnic meat markets, banks and credit unions, restaurants, and a small movie theater. (Photo: Gerda Wekerle)

SIDEWALK WIDTH

☐ Is the width of the sidewalk adequate for walking a comfortable distance from both buildings and the street?

☐ Can the sidewalk accommodate outdoor tables?

If sidewalk cafés are blocking the sidewalk, perhaps the answer is to widen the sidewalk, not ban the cafés.

Figure 4-45. Pedestrian zones have been popular in European cities. In Paris's Les Halles neighborhood, this pedestrian zone is thronged with shoppers and sightseers. In North American cities, including Ottawa and Vancouver, permanent pedestrian zones have resulted in the decline of commercial strips. New York City is experimenting with closing certain streets for specific hours of the day to encourage traffic calming and encourage pedestrian traffic. (Photo: Gerda Wekerle)

CONTINUITY TO STREET EDGE

☐ Are street-front buildings built up to a continuous setback line, thus eliminating dead spaces and entrapment spots adjacent to the sidewalk?

ENTRAPMENT SPOTS

☐ Are recessed, below- and above-grade entrances clearly visible from the street and well lit?

ABMS

☐ Do Automated Banking Machines (ABMs) have their entrances on commercial streets?

☐ Are they visible from the street, at street level, and adequately lit?

Entrances to ABMs should not be adjacent to bus stops, which could allow criminals to loiter near an entrance by pretending they are waiting for a bus.

NIGHT USE

☐ Is the night use of streets encouraged through a mix of commercial uses with different closing hours?

Some commercial streets include bookstores and convenience stores that are open late, movie theaters and restaurants, in addition to retail uses. If a bar is the only commercial use that is open until 1 A.M., perhaps a convenience store or a restaurant can be encouraged to remain open later.

Shopping Plazas: The Problem

Shopping plazas are increasingly experienced as unsafe. Suburban shopping malls are favorite places for car thefts. Large regional shopping plazas with parking lots for thousands of cars have recently been the sites of carjackings, where car owners were abducted along with their stolen cars. Both women and young children have been abducted from suburban shopping malls amidst the coming and going of thousands of other consumers.

Because they provide virtually the only public space in many suburban communities, shopping malls are the favorite spot for teenagers to hang out and this can result in intimidation for other users. Shopping malls also attract increasing numbers of the homeless. In many cities, shopping mall owners have invoked trespass laws to get rid of both teenagers and homeless people. This merely displaces the problem and ignores the central fact that malls are often the "town center" of suburban communities. Some malls have taken a more innovative and humane approach. At Dufferin Mall in Toronto, the mall manager responded to the large number of youth hanging out by providing empty stores to the school system for dropouts, contributing to the salary of youth workers, and subsidizing summer park programs. Mall merchants provide employment for youths involved in co-op education programs. The mall also funds a youth theater program and athletic teams. Space has also been provided for social services in the mall.

Many retail businesses have fled U.S. inner city areas. A few developers are experimenting with high-security retail centers in high-crime areas.[13] The emphasis is on security design and security hardware and costs are high. Typically, the entire site is enclosed by a six- to eight-foot high iron fence with a small number of remote-controlled gates. Infrared motion detectors and closed circuit TV cameras monitor the entire center, including the fence and loading docks. Lighting levels are three to five times the industry standard. A security command post located in a second-story retail space has a view of the entire center. A local police substation may also occupy space donated by the center. Round-the-clock security personnel account for 60 to 70 percent of common area charges at high-security shopping centers, compared with an industry average of about 15 percent. The development of high-security shopping centers in previously redlined center city areas has depended on both public sector funding and substantial community consultation and support. Cities have invested in street improvements, public services, bus reroutings, clean-up campaigns, better schools, and additional law enforcement. Local communities have been involved in issues of project design, store selection, minority ownership and employment practices. These projects are viewed as successful because they are used. But they are often perceived as the only secure public space in the community.[14]

Shopping Plazas: What to Look For

(Check the items that apply to each site.)

PARKING LOTS

☐ Do large parking lots in shopping malls have good signage so patrons can locate their cars quickly?

☐ Can large lots be sectioned into smaller lots that are less confusing?

☐ Are there signs advising patrons to lock cars?

☐ Are there emergency telephones?

☐ Are large lots monitored by video camera or regularly patrolled?

☐ Are bus stops located at the entrance of buildings rather than at the periphery of parking lots?

☐ Can parking lots be overlooked by store windows?

Figure 4-46. Shopping plazas, such as this Toronto example, were favored in the post-war era. Their characteristic large parking lots and inward-turning stores drain streets of vitality and create isolated spots for shoppers and employees at off-peak hours. This mall has become noted for its innovative youth programs and community partnerships have increased the use of the mall and adjacent neighborhood park. (Photo: Vincenzo Pietropaolo)

Figure 4-47. Suburban shopping centers are designed to turn inward and rarely have windows overlooking parking lots. This parking lot, located on the sides and back of a shopping mall, was the site of a sexual assault when a woman took a shortcut to a bus stop in the early morning hours. (Photo: Gerda Wekerle)

Figures 4-48, 4-49, 4-50. A typical configuration of "toilet-in-mall" planning. The toilet in this Brisbane, Australia, mall is tucked away in a corner of the mall, and accessed through an isolated corridor. Just off the entrance to the toilet is an open fire exit, which provides an ideal entrapment spot. (Photos: Carolyn Whitzman)

SERVICES

☐ Are there activities provided for youth, e.g., drop-in centers, libraries?

☐ Do activities such as mall walking programs attract a diverse group of users at different time periods?

☐ Does the design accommodate multiservice centers?

ENHANCED SECURITY IN HIGH-CRIME AREAS

☐ In high-crime areas, does planning, design, and financing reflect the additional costs of security?

☐ Are lighting levels three to five times the industry standards?

☐ Are there fences to close off the shopping center at off-hours to prevent use of public areas for criminal activity?

☐ Are there regular security patrols?

☐ Do police have a presence with a local substation?

☐ Do closed-circuit cameras monitor all common public areas, including loading docks?

☐ Is the community involved in defining security needs and solutions?

Industrial Areas: The Problem

Industrial areas become virtually deserted after work hours. Public transit is often limited. In older industrial areas, little thought has been given to the personal security of workers.

Figure 4-51. These transparent elevators, operating between the shopping and parking levels at Toronto's Eaton Center, avoid the sense of entrapment often felt in elevators and create opportunities for surveillance by passersby. (Photo: Vincenzo Pietropaolo)

Yet these are often the areas where people are employed in occupations involving shift work. These areas may also be dangerous due to numerous service alleyways, docks, and general physical neglect.

In cities such as New York, Seattle, Portland, San Francisco, Toronto, and Vancouver, industrial areas in prime locations near waterfronts are under pressure from gentrification, either for conversion to boutiques or restaurants or into loft living spaces. Special attention must be paid to urban safety measures, particularly in the early stages of conversion to new uses. Residents often move into existing industrial areas where the infrastructure does not yet support residential uses: Public transportation is limited or nonexistent, empty warehouses present dangers, and stores or services are not yet available.

Suburban industrial parks present new problems. They are car oriented, reached by curvilinear streets ending in cul-de-sacs, surrounded by parking lots. Loading docks are often hidden out of sight. For workers without cars, this type of design necessitates long walks from the nearest bus stop on an arterial road. Many spaces are hidden, isolated, and devoid of people or activities. These spaces attract illicit activities such as drug dealing or become hangouts for teenagers at night and on weekends.

Industrial Areas: What to Look For

(Check the items that apply to each site.)

LIGHTING

☐ Is pedestrian-scale lighting along streets and entrance paths to buildings equal to that found in commercial and residential areas?

☐ Is lighting focused to illuminate entrapment areas such as the entrances to loading docks?

☐ Do signs encourage reporting of burned-out or vandalized lights?

SIGHTLINES

☐ Is the parking lot visible from the street?

☐ Are parking lots and the paths to parking lots and transit stops visible from the buildings they serve?

☐ Are transit stops located as close as possible to buildings rather than isolated at the edge of a parking lot or only on arterial roads?

☐ Are loading docks overlooked by windows?

FORMAL SURVEILLANCE

☐ Can parking lots and transit stops be made visible from the workstations of building security personnel?

☐ Can an escort service or buddy system be created for late-night staff?

☐ Can buses, cabs, and other vehicles with radios be used to help keep an eye on the area?

☐ Is there place for a taxi stand?

Figure 4-52. Industrial areas combine uses such as auto body shops, closed-down warehouses, and loading docks. They are often isolated, poorly lit, and not well serviced by public transportation. Shift workers and suppliers need to feel that they will be safe in getting to and from work. (Photo: Joyce Brown)

Figure 4-53. This bus shelter in an industrial area is poorly sited beside an open field with broken fencing and under an expressway ramp. The location is isolated, with very little pedestrian or auto traffic. (Photo: Joyce Brown)

Figure 4-54. This renovation of an industrial building in Portland, Oregon, into stores and offices has kept the building and the area from declining. (Photo: Gerda Wekerle)

LAND USE MIX AND INTENSIFICATION

☐ Can empty parking lots be locked when not in use?

☐ In the early stages of gentrification or conversion, has thought been given to locate bus routes or bus stops in areas with maximum activity?

☐ Can temporary activities be planned to maintain a steady stream of people to make the area less isolated?

☐ In suburban industrial parks, does the zoning and design accommodate a range of uses, e.g., cafés and restaurants, mailbox operations, consumer services?

RESIDENTIAL AREAS

Safe residential areas are perhaps the most important element of safe cities. There is often a choice involved in avoiding an unsafe downtown, unsafe public transportation, or unsafe parks. For many people, especially many women, there is little choice in where to live. For the fortunate, home is a refuge from other stresses. For those being abused in their homes, or those afraid of the threat immediately outside their doors, "home" is the source of their most extreme stress.

Relatively well-to-do people in North America have gone to extraordinary lengths to make their homes feel safe from outside threats. The wholesale flight of the middle class from some inner cities has been one result of fear of crime. Lower-income housing complexes, public and private, are forced to resort to private security guards to police their grounds. Even in suburban neighborhoods, locked high fences, intercom entry systems, security patrols, and video surveillance have become elements of some middle- and high-income residential complexes. The security offered by these measures, however, can only be seen as illusory: voluntary incarceration in a kind of prison (with many security elements having been developed in prison settings) in order to avoid violence. Clearly, this kind of housing is inimical to the planning and design that will enhance city dwellers' lives.

Traditionally, residential areas were not separate from the main life of cities. The 19th century saw increasing division between women's realm (the home) and men's realm (the workplace) express itself in the development of suburbs. Increasing land use separation also affected public housing, which began as small projects and grew to larger and larger warehouses for the poor. Undeveloped green space was left in both suburbs and public housing projects for "recreation," ignoring the fact that children are less likely to play in undifferentiated green space than in places with inherent interest. Recent years have seen increased interest in "neo-traditional" planning, a return to smaller-scale, mixed-use projects. The problems of residential areas, therefore, can be loosely divided into those related to more traditional street-oriented developments and those related to extensive "super-block" residential developments.

Residential Streets: The Problem

Some residential streets are considered very unsafe by neighborhood residents. Of particular concern are streets with land uses that provide additional security risks, such as school yards, parking lots, construction sites, derelict buildings, or unfenced properties. Super-blocks with pedestrian-only streets create a fortress effect that limits informal surveillance by residents and nonresidents alike. While the introduction of public access streets is often opposed by residents who do not want to lose traffic safety, if the redevelopment is accompanied by intensification of shops and services that assist residents and might attract nonresidents, the benefits can outweigh the costs.

Another controversy associated with residential streets is on-street parking. Next to securable garages, on-street parking is the choice for many car owners. The safety concerns about people lurking in or next to parked cars must be balanced with the concern about parking in relatively isolated alleyways, lots, or garages. On-street parking can also limit the speed and number of cars, which in turn can make using the street safer from a traffic safety perspective.

Residential Streets: What to Look For

(Check the items that apply to each site.)

LIGHTING

☐ Is lighting sufficient to see a person approaching at a distance of 15 feet?

☐ Is the lighting sufficient for the sidewalk as well as the street?

☐ Can small signs be added to the fixtures, informing where to report repairs?

☐ Are trees and bushes trimmed adequately so as not to shade the fixtures?

LANEWAYS

☐ Are entrances to alleys or laneways well lit and clearly visible from the street?

CONTINUITY AND CLEAR OWNERSHIP

☐ If there are "gaps" in the street such as school yards or empty lots where an assailant can pull a passerby into an isolated area, are these made priorities for lighting, fencing, and possible redevelopment?

INFORMAL SURVEILLANCE AND ACTIVITY GENERATORS

☐ Are there opportunities for informal surveillance on the street, through the erection of porches and balconies, small convenience stores, or community gardens?

Figure 4-55. Porches on a residential street in Toronto allow informal surveillance in the summer. Encouraging the porch lights to be left on overnight is an important way to get more pedestrian-scale lighting. (Photo: Vincenzo Pietropaolo)

Figure 4-56. Providing space in residential areas for casual outdoor activities like washing the car helps to bring people out on to the street. (Photo: Gerda Wekerle)

☐ Does the street provide opportunities for children's play areas to be visible from their homes?

☐ Are there places on the street where adults can clean cars, sit on benches, or engage in other casual social and recreational activities?

WIDENING OF SIDEWALKS

☐ Where excessive car traffic is affecting casual use of the street during the day and the evening, is it possible to reduce car traffic and facilitate pedestrian use through the widening of sidewalks or solutions such as Dutch woonerfs which restrict car speed by adding obstructions to the street?

RESIDENTIAL STREET PATTERN

☐ Is the layout of new residential streets predictable?

☐ Can the streets be linked to an existing grid and pattern of streets?

☐ Would a stranger entering a street know how to get out?

Figure 4-57. Residential streets, where car traffic is restricted but not eradicated, are common in the Netherlands and in Scandinavia. They allow on-street car and bicycle parking, and open up the entire street surface to children's play. They're a success socially, environmentally, and from the standpoint of safety. (Photo: Gerda Wekerle)

Figure 4-58. This "woonerf" or "living street" in a suburban development near Delft, the Netherlands, is designed to slow local traffic and allow space for safe children's play and other domestic activities. (Photo: Gerda Wekerle)

Figure 4-59. Internal pedestrian pathways, segregating cars from pedestrians, and block towers are the hallmarks of this social housing project built in the 1970s. These internal pathways are difficult to police and create mazes that confuse residents and visitors alike. The hidden areas attract illegal activities. (Photo: Gerda Wekerle)

Figure 4-60. Private roads, rather than public streets, were popular in suburban developments built in the 1970s. In this Dutch example, house entrances face a narrow private road, almost a pathway. The small buildings to the left are storage lockers, out in the open, rather than hidden in a basement or out-of-the way space. (Photo: Gerda Wekerle)

Figure 4-61. In-fill housing in Regina, Saskatchewan, has shared parking in the rear, overlooked from the houses. (Photo: Gerda Wekerle)

The pattern, found in many North American suburbs, of unconnected cul-de-sacs can be very confusing to pedestrians trying to find their way. The traditional grid street pattern is preferable: short blocks and predictable layout lessen the possibility of entrapment spots, and allow familiar and unfamiliar users to understand their surroundings in a more comfortable way.

ON-STREET PARKING

☐ Is on-street parking a possibility, especially for residents who commonly work late and may be afraid to use other alternatives?

Alleys and Laneways: The Problem

Laneways and alleyways off or behind residential and commercial streets are often isolated spots, poorly lit and maintained. Many traditionally planned streets have alley parking. At best, these alleys become places where children can play sports and explore away from traffic safety concerns. At worst, alleys become unsafe and unsupervised places that provide criminal access to houses. Some cities, including San Francisco and Toronto, have explored ways to make laneways an amenity space. In new developments, back lanes are often preferable to front-of-the-house garages for parking access. Some new developments have created wider back lanes to provide a small courtyard that is used by residents and their children. In built-up areas of cities, new in-fill housing has been built with rear lane access.

Alleys and Laneways: What to Look For

(Check the items that apply to each site.)

LIGHTING

☐ Is lighting of laneways or alleys of the same quality as the street lighting?

In the case of public laneways, this is the responsibility of the municipal government. Where there are private laneways, the owner is responsible.

SIGHTLINES / AVOIDING ENTRAPMENT

☐ Are laneways straight, with more than one entrance?

Laneways that take a sharp turn should be equipped with angled mirrors. Laneways that dead end should be avoided, when possible. Existing dead-end laneways can sometimes be extended as part of a redevelopment.

MAINTENANCE

☐ Is maintenance of public and private alleys strictly enforced?

Graffiti and refuse in alleys and laneways gives the impression of incivility. Of particular concern are abandoned cars and open garages and sheds in laneways.

☐ Are garage doors shut to avoid entrapment spots?

Figure 4-62. A small café courtyard livens up a laneway in this Toronto midtown commercial district. Laneways that are often used as shortcuts can be transformed into pedestrian streets with the cooperation of neighboring business. (Photo: Vincenzo Pietropaolo)

Figure 4-63. This vest-pocket park behind a city-owned market in Toronto was formerly a parking lot in an alley. It is overlooked by housing on the left and warehouses on the right. (Photo: Gerda Wekerle)

Figure 4-64. This wide alleyway in Toronto became the site of a small in-fill housing project with doors facing the alley. (Photo: Gerda Wekerle)

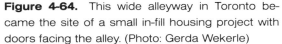

INTENSIFICATION

☐ Where housing and work sheds can be built in laneways, is the entrance to laneway housing visible from the street, or failing that, from the windows of other buildings?

ADDING ACTIVITIES

☐ Is it possible to transform alleys into pedestrian streets or linear parks?

School Yards: The Problem

School yards have become sites for drug dealing, sexual assaults, and often become hangouts for teenagers after school hours. Many school yards have environmental characteristics that make a place less safe: They are off a major pedestrian route, deserted after school hours, relatively isolated, often fenced in with few escape routes, and not visible from the street. They are frequently the only public space in a residential area and attract many potential users and activities. Portable classrooms in school yards have been identified as new urban safety problems. They can be more easily entered by people coming off the street and place both teachers and students at greater risk.

School Yards: What to Look For

(Check the items that apply to each site.)

LOCATION OF SCHOOL YARDS

☐ Are school yards entirely visible from the street, rather than tucked behind the school?

☐ Are portable classrooms visible from the main building and the street?

FORMAL SURVEILLANCE

☐ Is there supervised recreation after school hours?

☐ Are there security patrols?

INTENSIFICATION OF LAND USE

☐ Is it possible to incorporate other activities, such as community gardens or bocci/handball courts, to bring people into the school yard in off-hours?

Some schools regularly hold flea markets and community garage sales to bring uses into the yards and raise funds.

Figure 4-65. A Minneapolis–St.Paul school yard is open to view from the adjoining streets and houses and does not have hidden and isolated spaces behind the school. (Photo: Mary deLaittre)

Figure 4-66. By installing a community garden, new activities and users are introduced into this center block school yard that is the size of two football fields. Students tend the raised beds during the school year; a senior's group takes over in the summer. Gardening brings neighborhood residents into the school yard in the evenings and on weekends and has driven out drug dealing and teenage drinking parties. (Photo: Gerda Wekerle)

Figure 4-67. A school yard on New York's Upper East Side that is fenced and locked on weekends and at night. While this is a solution to illegal activities, it makes valuable community open space unavailable for play and community activities. (Photo: Gerda Wekerle)

LOCKING AND SIGNAGE

☐ After dark or when school yards are not supervised, are yards locked and signage placed that states the penalties for trespassing?

☐ Are unused areas fenced?

LIGHTING

☐ Is the school yard well lit, especially where it is adjacent to a residential area?

Extensive High-rise Residential Areas: The Problem

Extensive high-rise residential areas tend to have one or more of the following characteristics: a high percentage of "empty" or largely unused space; separation into large zones that are exclusively used for driving, walking, parking, shopping, or recreation; poor signage and related sense of "placelessness"; limited opportunities for natural surveillance; and a sense of isolation. These problems are often exacerbated in lower-income areas, where maintenance may be poor to nonexistent and formal surveillance limited. In many large public housing projects built in the 1960s, drug dealers have taken over courtyards, internal walkways, and, in some cities, entire buildings.

Many American and European designers have turned their attention to low-income high-rise residential areas, among them, Oscar Newman[15] and Alice Coleman.[16] They have proposed changes in physical design to reduce crime, including enclosing spaces with gates and fences, limiting the number of households sharing an entrance, eliminating internal walkways, and adding security hardware. Criticisms of such design solutions include the possibility that expensive design "solutions" will lead to the eviction or replacement of present lower-income residents. The reliance on security hardware has sometimes been viewed as a one-shot solution that worked against the implementation of management changes and community crime prevention initiatives. In public and private low income high rises alike, there has been a tendency to impose "top-down" decisions without adequate consultation with the neighborhood.

The first principle when considering extensive high-rise residential areas is to avoid them. They are inherently problematic from the perspective of personal safety; they also are questionable from environmental and social perspectives.

Extensive High-Rise Residential Areas: What to Look For

(Check the items that apply to each site.)

LIGHTING

☐ Are pedestrian pathways leading to buildings lit to public street standards (4 footcandles at face height)?

☐ Do the lights shine on the sidewalk while avoiding the lower floors of buildings?

☐ Are there signs indicating where to report maintenance problems?

Figure 4-68. Public housing in the 1960s was often built as tower blocks with interior courtyards. In this Toronto project, the courtyard became the site of a sexual assault. Courtyards are also used for drug dealing and residents must run a gauntlet to get into their units. One solution is to run a street grid through the projects to open up the private roads and semipublic hidden spaces to casual passersby and police patrols. (Photo: Gerda Wekerle)

SAFE ROUTES

☐ Do essential routes through the area provide clear sightlines, as opposed to a series of controlled "picturesque" views?

☐ Is it possible to promote activity that will result in more eyes on the street along these routes, including the reintroduction of public roads?

Priorities for safe routes include the routes leading to and from transit stops, parking lots, and shopping areas. It is easier to provide safe routes when the streets adjacent to the high-rise buildings are public.

☐ Are especially vulnerable groups, such as older people, located near essential services such as stores or public transit so they avoid "running the gauntlet"?

Locate people with mobility impairments, including some elderly, near services and locate families with young children near playgrounds. This is not only for ease of access, but also avoids "running the gauntlet" past teenage hangouts.

INTENSIFICATION

☐ Is it possible to fill in "empty" space, especially at grade, with human scale housing, commercial and community services that are complementary to the needs of the existing residents?

☐ Is it possible to create community gardens, school farms, or workshops on little-used land or are these already present?

PRIVATIZATION

☐ Is it possible to allocate part of the space to individual households to use as yards or gardens (if residents agree)?

Figure 4-69. When buildings are boarded up, they create dead spaces. These boarded-up buildings used by drug dealers on New York City's Lower East Side have recently been renovated, through a home-steading program, and occupied. (Photo: Marlis Momber)

Figure 4-70. This empty lot with garbage, burned-out cars, and falling-down buildings, on New York City's Lower East Side, creates an image of a war zone and a danger to neighborhood residents. Low-cost housing has recently been built on this site. (Photo: Marlis Momber)

Figure 4-71. Suburban high-rise developments built in the 1960s left substantial grassed areas around the buildings. The play area is isolated from both the buildings and the street and no one takes ownership of this space. (Photo: Gerda Wekerle)

Figure 4-72. This playground at the center of a social housing project in Toronto is surrounded on three sides by nonprofit housing cooperatives whose windows overlook the play area. (Photo: Gerda Wekerle)

FORMAL SURVEILLANCE

☐ Through strategic location of central management offices and/or training of management staff to respond to emergencies, are there formal "eyes on the street" during the day and evening?

☐ Do the police or private security patrol this area?

☐ Are residents encouraged to provide surveillance and report suspicious activity?

SIGNAGE

☐ Are street numbers visible from the public road and are there site maps at central locations for visitors, delivery people, and emergency services?

ACCESS TO INDIVIDUAL BUILDINGS

☐ Are entrances to individual buildings clearly visible from adjacent streets?

☐ Are entrances locked?

SPACE TO ORGANIZE

☐ Does management have explicit security policies that allow for improving the quality of the environment and fostering a sense of common purpose?

☐ Is there meeting space or a community center so that residents can organize and involve themselves in defining the problems and creating solutions?

Interior Spaces in Multiunit Housing: The Problem

Stairwells, laundry rooms, elevators, and entrances to buildings are often cited by residents as sites of assaults. What these places have in common is isolation and poor sightlines. Maintenance is another concern. The provision of entrance doors with intercoms will only accomplish its purpose if intercoms work and door locks are replaced when damaged. Improper tenant education also results in misuse of security features, such as lobby doors being propped open or not asking who is at the other end of an intercom before buzzing them in.

Security-conscious design is not the complete answer to improving security in multistory housing. Ongoing process issues, including tenant involvement in choosing and maintaining security features, housing allocation, staff/tenant relations, and inter-tenant conflict resolution, are security issues that need to be on the table when a safety strategy is being discussed for a building. This is especially true for new buildings: A security strategy needs to be developed before problems begin. In some cities, designers have begun to expand their comments beyond the exterior of new multiunit apartment buildings into interior common spaces. Other actors, such as architects, developers, and future residents (if known), need to give these spaces careful consideration before problems begin.

Interior of Multiunit Housing: What to Look For

(Check the items that apply to each site.)

LIGHTING

☐ Is lighting of common areas such as corridors, entrances, elevators, and stairwells adequate?

☐ Are areas of shadow avoided through use of more lighting fixtures?

SIGHTLINES

☐ Do key routes, such as routes from parking and the laundry room to elevators, provide clear sightlines?

☐ Is the lobby visible from the interior of the building or the street?

☐ Would use of transparent materials and security mirrors improve sightlines?

ELEVATOR SIGHTLINES

☐ Is the interior of an elevator mirrored or does it have an angled mirror if the entire interior area is not visible to a person about to enter?

LOCATION OF ACTIVITY GENERATORS

☐ Are activity generators, such as party rooms and laundry rooms, near entrances to make both spaces safer?

INFORMAL SURVEILLANCE OF LAUNDRY ROOM AND PLAY AREAS

☐ Can laundry rooms be viewed from the street, the entrance, or some other source of informal surveillance?

Figure 4-73. Stairwells in high-rise buildings can be dangerous places where residents are mugged and drug dealing occurs. This multistory building in London, England, placed the glass-enclosed stairwell in the front for maximum security. (Photo: Gerda Wekerle)

Figure 4-74. In a building owned and operated by the YWCA of Metropolitan Toronto, the front door is overlooked by staff offices and other entrances are also overlooked by windows to increase passive surveillance. (Photo: Gerda Wekerle)

Figure 4-75. This staggered hallway may break down the institutional feeling of long hallways but it creates uncertainty and hiding places. (Photo: Sandra Colangelo)

☐ Are outdoor play areas visible from apartments, preferably from kitchens or living rooms?

LOCKING DEVICES

☐ Are interior door locks at least a one inch (25 mm) dead bolt?

☐ Are glass panels near doors reinforced or eliminated?

☐ Are windows lockable from the inside?

☐ Are French doors equipped with bars?

☐ Do garden gates lock?

☐ Are door locks changed every time there is a change in tenants?

FORMAL SURVEILLANCE

☐ Do superintendents, maintenance staff, or residents patrol halls, parking garages or lots, and other common areas?

☐ Do they know how to report maintenance problems and how to respond in an emergency?

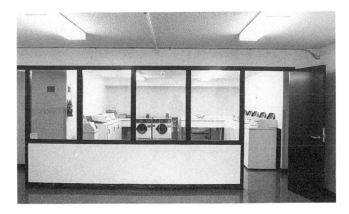

Figure 4-76. View of the laundry room of the Oak Street Housing Co-operative, Toronto, from the entrance to the apartment building. The room adjacent to the laundry is used for meetings or as a playroom for children while parents are doing laundry. (Photo: Vincenzo Pietropaolo)

Figure 4-77. Laundry rooms are often relegated to the basement of apartment buildings. Usually isolated and dark, tenants are reluctant to use them. In this building, developed by a women's organization, a high priority was a ground floor laundry room overlooking the front lobby of the building. (Photo: Sandra Colangelo)

Figure 4-78. Storage lockers are often located in basements, isolated, and dimly lit. Tenants may find their lockers vandalized and that items are stolen from such out-of-the way spaces. (Photo: Robert Stamenov)

Figure 4-79 Storage lockers in the open, adjacent to a main pathway, and attractively screened with vines. Note the portholes in the doors for added security. (Photo: Gerda Wekerle)

Parks: The Problem

Historically, parks have been viewed as oases and sanctuaries from urban life. Increasingly, however, urban parks, from small neighborhood parks to larger regional parks, generate fear and avoidance. In some cities, neighborhoods have organized to keep out new parks for fear that they will become sites of criminal activity. Parks are contested urban space. Some urban parks have become "hot spots" of crime, attracting drug dealing and other illicit activities and experiencing a downward spiral that drives away a diversity of users and activities. In many cities, parks have become the sites of gay bashing and even homicides of gay men. Incidents involving sexual violence against women in parks are widely publicized. The attack on a female jogger in Central Park in New York City by a youth gang received international press coverage.

The design of parks has not kept pace with current concerns about urban crime. Many parks departments do not address urban safety issues in park design. Most cities have not developed security programs for parks. New York City has been a leader in parks security programs, and other cities, such as Toronto and Chicago, are giving priority to developing security programs for urban parks.[17]

Traditionally, parks have been designed to turn their back on the city through the use of buffers that surround the park and protect it from noise, traffic, and surrounding buildings.[18] Yet this design philosophy creates areas of concealment, prevents users from seeing what is around them, and limits escape routes. The uncertainty this instills in park users creates a sense of fear and results in lower park usage.

The recent interest within the landscape profession and among parks planners in increasing the biodiversity of sites by naturalizing open areas may also contribute to higher levels of fear in parks.[19] It is paradoxical that the types of open spaces that are most valued—woodlands, shrub thickets, and tall grass meadows—are also viewed as high-risk areas by the general public, and especially by women.[20] Because naturalized areas provide a confined field of view and are often isolated, people are more apprehensive and tend to avoid them more.

Another issue related to urban safety in parks is framed as the collapse of collective care and responsibility.[21] Due to the ambiguity of ownership in open spaces, people are particularly sensitive to antisocial behavior, such as teenage delinquency, vandalism, sexual violence, and racial attacks in parks. Women from minority communities feel particularly at risk in unsupervised parks. In some communities, reclaiming the neighborhood park or playground has become the focus of activities to clean up the block.[22]

Those groups who are most dependent on urban nature areas tend to display the greatest levels of insecurity in parks: women, children, the elderly, the physically handicapped, and visible minority groups. When fear of crime in urban parks hinders their use, this becomes an issue of access and equity. In one study of a large regional park in Toronto, for example, researchers found that twice as many males as females used the park in the daytime and three times as many men as women used it at night.[23] Fear of crime was a major reason given by women for nonusage of the park. In response, local women's groups developed their own proposals to make this park a place where women will feel more secure. These proposals have been incorporated into the new master plan proposals for the park and a security working group, which includes local women's groups, is developing a plan for the park.

New York City has pioneered programs to make parks safer through positive use.[24] Citizen and private sector involvement has been assured through a system of community boards and the encouragement of 500 active volunteer groups, including groups that clean up parks. Effective design for security has the objective of creating secure, maintainable environments so that users will feel comfortable in parks. Attention has been paid to design that will allow users to find their way easily, see potential dangers quickly, and move freely without barriers.

A high priority has been the removal of signs of physical and social incivility, such as graffiti and litter. A new program puts homeless people, some of whom live in the parks, to work picking up litter on the perimeter of Central Park.[25]

The parks department has also dramatically improved security in high-profile projects such as Union Square and Bryant Park. Union Square, on New York's lower east side, was a drug haven and a blot on the neighborhood. Through partnership with local community groups, the park was redesigned to eliminate hiding places and places of entrapment. This meant minimizing walls and changes in elevation, creating clear and effective sightlines and circulation, and broadening entrances. Activities were moved to the active edges of the park and a Green Market was introduced two days a week. In addition, a Parks Enforcement Officer provides a continuous presence in the park. Changes to Bryant Park, located behind the New York City Public Library, have had a similar focus. Priority was given to eliminating shrubbery, fences, and elevations that separated the park from the surrounding street and that enclosed and sheltered criminal activities. Space was made for cappuccino bars, a half-price Broadway tickets kiosk, and activities such as concerts in the park. A well-tended sunny lawn and movable chairs attract thousands of people at lunch hours. In these parks and others, park planners have devoted a great deal of attention to programming to encourage active use and to attract a range of users. In addition, direct security has been provided by Parks Security Police and Urban Park Rangers in Central Park who provide educational programs as well as eyes on the park.

Parks: What to Look For[26]

(Check the items that apply to each site.)

LIGHTING

☐ Is lighting in public outdoor spaces adequate to get a good look at another person a reasonable distance, i.e., 12 to 15 feet, away?

☐ Are landscaping elements chosen and maintained so that they do not block the light?

☐ Is lighting placed where nighttime activity is appropriate and not placed in areas that would be inherently unsafe or that are not intended to be used at night?

☐ If the park is intended for night use, are the paths and potential entrapment areas lit to street level?

☐ Are there programmed nighttime activities, such as night baseball games or evening nature walks, that bring people into the park after dark?

☐ Are nighttime activities clustered?

☐ Do nighttime activity nodes take advantage of nighttime activities and street life such as nearby restaurants and movie theaters?

☐ Are principal access routes to nighttime activity nodes identified and is their use encouraged?

☐ Are nighttime corridors properly illuminated so that potential hiding areas are illuminated?

☐ Are nighttime routes made more visible by improving sightlines to them and by giving priority to patrols?

☐ In larger parks, is there a buddy system or a jogging club to ensure the safety of joggers at off-hours?

Parks are underutilized during evening hours even though this is when many potential users have discretionary time. Not all areas of parks can be made safe for nighttime activities. Nature trails pose security problems. Lighting nature trails would also interfere with the wildlife and plants that are very sensitive to changes in photoperiod.

Closing parks at night is more a tradition in European cities than in North American

Figure 4-80. Pedestrian-level lighting in Central Park, New York City. Well-signed emergency telephones are being installed in some areas of the park. Maintenance is important, as this phone has been vandalized. (Photo: David Orsini)

cities. In Paris and Amsterdam, major urban parks are locked after dusk. In New York, small vest-pocket parks in the downtown are locked with a gate. Most community gardens have gates and are locked at night. There is considerable debate as to whether urban parks should be fenced and locked at night. Some people argue that this will attract antisocial activities and create dead space that keeps out law-abiding residents.

SIGHTLINES

☐ Is it possible to see most of a small park or play area from the street?

☐ Are small parks or the edges of larger parks overlooked by housing or commercial establishments?

Figure 4-81 A city park in the Netherlands has gates that are locked at night. (Photo: Carolyn Whitzman)

☐ Do pathways have unimpeded sightlines, especially where they curve or change grade, so that people can see into and out of an area?

☐ Are landscape materials chosen and maintained so that they do not block sightlines from the street or along paths?

MOVEMENT PREDICTORS

☐ Do people have a choice of routes to and from areas of the park?

☐ Is there more than one entrance or exit, especially when there is a fence around a play area or a vest-pocket park?

☐ Are there anchors of activity located near movement predictors, where appropriate?

An important aspect of open space design is sequential movement. Pedestrians meander through areas with changing sightlines and spaces may open up and contract. Especially when people have limited choice of routes, it is important that park design provide good sightlines and visual permeability, as well as multiple exit and access points. The absence of alternative routes results in channelized movement so that assailants can predict behavior and lie in wait for victims.

ENTRAPMENT SPOTS

☐ Do pathways have a border of low-lying or high-branching vegetation, as opposed to trees and bushes that can easily create entrapment spots?

Figure 4-82. All of the West Side Community Garden in New York City can be seen at a glance from the entrance adjacent to the sidewalk. The allotment garden behind the fence ensures constant surveillance by some of the 300 members who tend this garden. It is also overlooked by windows of adjoining housing. The sense of pride and ownership that neighborhood residents invest in this community garden make it a well-used space. (Photo: Gerda Wekerle)

Figure 4-83. An old-fashioned avenue in a new neighborhood, David Crombie Park in Toronto's St. Lawrence Neighborhood, developed on obsolete industrial lands in the core area. This linear park has good lighting, sightlines, and visibility from surrounding buildings. Linear parks and walking trails are newly popular in cities, but residents often try to block them for fear that they will attract strangers and criminal activities. Careful attention to design for personal safety could allay some of these fears. (Photo: Vincenzo Pietropaolo)

Figure 4-84. A pathway through the middle of Union Square in New York City encourages neighborhood residents to walk through the park, not around it. A new luxury condominium project recently built on one side of the Square was built only after the city gave assurances that the Square would be redeveloped to improve its safety. (Photo: David Orsini)

Figure 4-85. The Greenmarket, a farmer's market held at Union Square in New York City four days a week, attracts customers from all over New York, even in the winter months. The market is located in a parking lot, adjacent to a permanent newsstand, the subway entrance, and a children's playground. (Photo: Gerda Wekerle)

Figure 4-86. Fencing this children's playground in New York City's Riverside Park protects children from running off and defines a parent-and-child-only space, but the single exit also creates an entrapment area that could be dangerous. (Photo: Margaret Lander)

Figure 4-87. This small park on the Left Bank of Paris has a "garden" kiosk for a park attendant. These kiosks are common in Paris neighborhood parks. The constant presence of an attendant ensures greater safety for all users, but especially unattended children. (Photo: Gerda Wekerle)

☐ Are children's play structures designed to minimize entrapment spots in the play equipment or within a fenced area?

☐ Are toilets designed to eliminate hidden corners or entrapment areas?

SIGNAGE

☐ Does signage at entrances to the park provide a clear orientation to major points of interest?

☐ Does signage clearly indicate, using words, international symbols, and maps, the location of telephones, toilets, isolated trails, heavily used routes, and park activities?

☐ Are the signs located at decision points, such as the intersection of two major paths?

☐ Do area locators have a map of the area with an enlargement of the immediate area to indicate where a person is within the park and where the closest park headquarters and exit routes are located?

☐ Do the signs indicate where and how help can be found and where maintenance problems can be reported?

☐ Do the telephones have prominently displayed locator codes known to police and park personnel?

A signage system provides a park with a vital information network that is important to the legibility and image of the park. A park signage system should possess qualities of coherence and uniformity. Design should maximize the visibility of signage while minimizing the obtrusiveness of park signage. Within the park signage system, there should be information to enhance public awareness of safety in the park, including location of telephones and park headquarters and safety tips. The Parks Department should also produce a pamphlet dedicated to public awareness of park safety.

ISOLATION

☐ Is the park enclosed by shrubs and fences so that passersby cannot see into the park?

☐ Is the park above or below grade and hidden from the street?

☐ Is there an active edge that attracts activity and allows use without penetrating the park interior?

☐ Are there emergency telephones in isolated areas, including trails?

Where possible, some facilities and activity areas should be located near the perimeter of the park. Surveillance will be enhanced from the street as well as from the concentration of edge activities. An active edge encourages use and creates a perimeter of surveillance for the park. Major park activity nodes are often located in the interior of a park and not visible

Figure 4-88. New York City's Central Park provides marked lanes for joggers and rollerbladers. Pedestrians are well served by sidewalks and walking trails. This mix of activities and users contributes to the safety of the park. (Photo: Gerda Wekerle)

Figure 4-89. Central Park planners try to make the park safer by encouraging a range of programming, including the Central Park Summer Stage, Shakespeare in the Park programs, running clinics for joggers, and organized nature walks. (Photo: David Orsini)

Figure 4-90. This restaurant in a London, England, park attracts park users. (Photo: Carolyn Whitzman)

from the street. Users feel unsafe if they must cross uncontrolled, unobserved, and ambiguous space to reach park activities. Higher levels of activity on the edges of the park may serve to introduce users to the park. People who feel apprehension or have mobility problems can use these perimeter areas with clear sightlines to other users and activities.

LOCATION OF ACTIVITY GENERATORS

☐ Are activities located either along the edge of parks or clustered in nodes?

☐ Are children's playgrounds located near other activity generators such as food kiosks?

☐ In smaller parks or vest-pocket parks, does the design allow space for food kiosks?

Figure 4-91. The renovations to New York City's Bryant Park, behind the New York City Public Library, created two attractive food kiosks that serve pastries, snacks, and high-quality coffee. The park now attracts thousands of people at lunchtime. (Photo: Gerda Wekerle)

☐ Is flexible seating provided to allow people choice?

☐ Are toilets located near telephones?

☐ When siting a new toilet facility, is it located adjacent to existing activities?

☐ If a toilet is isolated, can it be moved?

MAINTENANCE

☐ Are there signs of physical incivility, e.g., garbage or graffiti?

☐ In naturalized areas, does a mown edge of three to four feet along a path or area adjacent to a naturalized landscape indicate that these areas are naturalized through intent rather than neglect?

☐ Where an area has deteriorated because its carrying capacity has been exceeded, can the environment be designed to be more resistant to deterioration or can activities be shifted to alternate sites to allow regeneration?

It is important that naturalized areas are seen to be under the care of parks personnel. Maintenance of trails and signage, and a visible staff presence increases the public's perception of safety in these areas. Because damaged areas and facilities have a negative impact on the park's image and spawn further damage and neglect, damaged areas should receive prompt attention. Park maintenance crews might be stationed in specific areas or "flying crews" designated to repair park damage swiftly.

Figure 4-92. Where there are naturalized areas in parks, park planners fear that the public's concern with safety will conflict with naturalizing efforts, forcing meadows to be cut and shrubs to be trimmed. Here, Central Park has mown a wide swath of grass adjacent to the pathway to enhance a feeling of safety. (Photo: David Orsini)

Figure 4-93. Especially in naturalized areas, good signage reassures users by allowing them to orient themselves. How can a park user know that a transit stop and a well-traveled road are less than fifty yards from this jogging trail? (Photo: Vincenzo Pietropaolo)

PLANNING FOR A RANGE OF ACTIVITIES AND A DIVERSITY OF USERS

☐ Do larger parks provide opportunities for leisure activities beyond team sports and children's play to attract a diversity of users? e.g., community gardens, small zoos or farms, puppet shows and plays, seniors' activities.

☐ Do park activities and design encourage a diversity of users or do some users take over the park and drive out other users?

☐ Are downtown parks designed to accommodate a range of activities, even if they are intended primarily for passive use? e.g., space for street vendors, street entertainers, concerts, picnics, food services, and green markets.

☐ Does programming of park activities accommodate a range of interests and park users?

Use of urban open space is often marked by competing interests and noncomplementary uses. The use of urban parks by the homeless often discourages other users. In some cities, mass evictions of the homeless from public parks have become commonplace. Yet these actions merely displace the homeless to other locations and deprive them of access to public environments. The greater the diversity of people and activities encouraged in an open space, the greater its publicness. Programming contributes to the safety of urban parks: Free events and concerts attract a diverse audience and introduce people to the park. Interpretive programming can inform visitors about the history of an area, urban ecology, and habitat restoration. Demonstrations and guided walks can enhance people's understanding and use of a park, and will increase security in remote areas.

FORMAL SURVEILLANCE

☐ Is formal surveillance of parks provided either by police or park personnel?

☐ Do park attendants know how to respond to emergencies?

☐ Are park staff given security training?

☐ Is there a safety plan for parks that incorporates printed matter, signage, and interpretive programming?

☐ Within the Parks Department, is there a Safety Officer responsible for safety throughout the parks system?

Maintaining park areas by way of zone gardeners instead of "flying squads" can introduce a continual human presence in an area. Gardeners attached to specific areas can quickly spot any departure from the normal life of the area and provide a familiar face to park users. Within the Parks Department, it is essential to develop clear accountability for security. Safety programs must be monitored and implemented. Data must be collected on the incidence of crime in parks and the profile of users in order to develop appropriate responses. Some cities have assigned parks personnel to security functions. New York City has a parks security police force and park rangers who provide interpretive programs as well as enforce bylaws. In cities where parks security is left to the police department, some cities have introduced police bicycle patrols.

Figure 4-94. Parks don't have to be segregated from housing. In this suburban social housing development near Delft, the Netherlands, open space adjacent to medium-density housing is naturalized and luxuriously landscaped. (Photo: Gerda Wekerle)

Figure 4-95. The stream attracts children for fishing and wading. Parents can oversee children's play from their units. In this case, naturalized plantings and urban safety complement one another. (Photo: Gerda Wekerle)

Figure 4-96. This facility, in a strip mall in a Toronto suburb, is only one of several private playgrounds that have recently opened up. Parents pay an hourly fee so that children can play in this supervised setting. As parents fear for their children's safety in parks, and neighborhood groups organize to keep new public parks out of residential areas due to fear of crime, such privatization of children's play will increase. (Photo: Gerda Wekerle)

PUBLIC AWARENESS OF SAFETY CONCERNS

☐ Are citizens involved and consulted about their use of parks and possible solutions to urban safety concerns?

☐ Is there a Park Watch program?

☐ Are shop owners and commercial building owners along the perimeter of parks involved in monitoring the park?

Community involvement is critical to a sense of ownership of parks. By opening up the planning, design, management, programming, and redesign of the park to the public, the park becomes truly public. Ongoing public consultation can occur through the establishment of a Citizens Advisory Committee. It might also involve a public awareness program that trains people to be observers and to report park incidents that might affect urban safety in parks. While natural surveillance is important to improving the safety of public open space, it must be combined with an awareness of what to observe, how to report breaches of security, and how and when to intervene. It is important that people are encouraged to report incidents of physical and social incivility, since it is the accumulation of incivilities that makes people avoid public spaces and contributes to fear of crime.

University and College Campuses: The Problem

Violence against persons is on the rise on many university and college campuses. Rapes and other forms of sexual assaults are a major threat to college students. A 1987 survey of 6000 students in 32 colleges across the United States found that one out of every six female students reported being a victim of rape or attempted rape during the preceding year.[27] The assaults occurred in residence halls, fraternity houses, parking lots, and libraries. The majority of the reported cases were "acquaintance rapes." Campuses are responding by establishing preventive education programs, increasing campus security, adopting new procedures, and providing victim assistance programs.

University and college campuses are often the size of small cities. Those developed in the 1960s follow the suburban model of ring roads, parking lots on the periphery of the campus, walking paths through wooded areas, and residences separated from classrooms and centers of activity. Many university campuses were designed to encourage access by the community: buildings have multiple entrances and exits, classrooms and common rooms are open until all hours of the night, labs run 24 hours of the day, and libraries have late closing hours. Such campuses are very difficult to monitor and limit access. In addition, the low-density, spread-out nature of many college campuses makes them difficult to police by campus security and increases campus users' fear of crime. Assaults on students are most likely to occur where they live, although students themselves report feeling least safe in areas with natural vegetation, areas with places to hide, and areas of poor lighting. Students feel more vulnerable in isolated areas. [28]

Responding to concerns about campus safety, universities and colleges have improved lighting, installed emergency telephones, set up escort services and campus transit services, and increased campus security personnel. Some universities and colleges have begun to involve all segments of the community in conducting safety audits of the campus and making recommendations for change. Increasingly, campus security departments publicize sexual assaults when they occur and alert the community. York University, for example, disseminates daily incident reports by e-mail. Changes in campus design, the assessment of the physical environment for possible unsafe areas, and changes in management style to focus on crime prevention and education can reduce fear and mitigate crime.

Post-secondary institutions have been unprepared for the increase in awareness of sexual assaults on campus and the fear it has engendered. Few colleges have in place a comprehensive program to deal with the increase in reported sexual assaults, particularly among acquaintances who continue to see one another in residence halls or classrooms. Colleges and universities are responding to the acquaintance rape problem through educational programs directed at students, faculty, and staff. Campuses have developed new policies on codes of conduct, disciplinary measures, and procedures to assist victims of sexual assault. Colleges and universities are also responding to the increased perception of danger on campuses by teaching crime prevention strategies and making changes in the physical environment.

Courts now hold universities responsible for criminal incidents if they are preventable. A recent act passed by the U.S. Congress, The Campus Crime Awareness and Campus Security Act of 1990, requires that colleges and universities publicly report crime statistics occurring on campus. In this way, the "duty to warn," to avoid civil liability, has created

Figure 4-97. Personal safety and access by people with disabilities were afterthoughts on many North American campuses built in the post-war period. Intensifying activities by adding a range of new buildings is one design solution. Attempting to channel evening traffic along relatively well-lit and well-traveled routes and providing frequent orientation points are other possibilities. This example of night walking routes is from the University of California, Berkeley. (Photo: Carolyn Whitzman)

an incentive for college administrators to put more resources into all aspects of campus safety.

Personal Safety on College Campuses: What to Look For

(Check the items that apply to each site or situation.)

CHOICE OF PATHS

☐ Do campus users have a choice of paths to get to essential buildings and services, including residences, lecture halls, cafeterias, and sports complexes?

☐ Is there enough space for pedestrians to move away from potential hiding places, especially at night?

LIGHTING

☐ Is lighting adequate (i.e., at least 4 footcandles) on footpaths, in parking lots, at entrances to buildings?

☐ Are there pools of light and darkness?

EMERGENCY TELEPHONES

☐ Are emergency telephones placed at strategic locations and connected directly to campus security?

☐ Are they easily identified either by a blue light, highly visible color, or signs?

PARKING LOTS / GARAGES

☐ Are parking lots relegated to the periphery of the campus?

☐ Are there options for parking closer to buildings after dark?

☐ Are there regular security patrols in the parking lots?

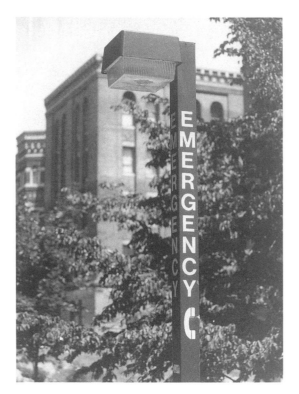

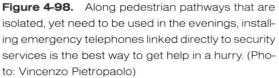

Figure 4-98. Along pedestrian pathways that are isolated, yet need to be used in the evenings, installing emergency telephones linked directly to security services is the best way to get help in a hurry. (Photo: Vincenzo Pietropaolo)

☐ Is there adequate signage in large surface parking lots so that users can find their car quickly?

☐ Are there emergency telephones located in the parking lots?

☐ Is there an escort service to the parking lots after dark?

☐ Are parking garages designed to maximize passive surveillance by placing glass stairwells in corners?

☐ In larger surface lots and garages, is surveillance provided through closed-circuit television?

ESCORT SERVICE

☐ Is there an evening escort service available on campus?

☐ Does it minimize waiting times to less than 15 minutes?

☐ Do the hours of operation match the times of operation of the library, labs, and campus pub?

☐ Are the personnel involved in the escort service trained to respond to women's fear of crime and are they adequately screened?

TRANSPORT SERVICES

☐ On large campuses, is there a shuttle bus to link far-flung parts of the campus?

☐ Does it link to rapid transit or major bus routes?

Figure 4-99. Emergency telephones on the University of Chicago campus spill over into Hyde Park, the adjacent neighborhood, where many students and faculty live. (Photo: Gerda Wekerle)

Figure 4-100. Many universities have set up campus escort services. The University of California, Berkeley, set up this service in the 1970s. (Photo: Gerda Wekerle)

Figure 4-101. This campus shuttle service at the University of California, Berkeley, operates between the rapid transit station and major university buildings. Many large urban universities, including UCLA, University of Wisconsin, Madison, and University of Minnesota, have set up university-funded transit services to increase campus safety. Some ride services operate throughout the day and night; others operate only after dark. In smaller cities, university ride services take students to their home. (Photo: Gerda Wekerle)

The University of Wisconsin, Madison, set up a Women's Transit Authority in 1973, providing a free shuttle bus between 7 P.M. and 2 A.M. seven days a week. This was fully funded by the university. The University of California, Berkeley, runs a shuttle bus to stops throughout the campus and to the rapid transit station in downtown Berkeley.

PATROLS

☐ Are there periodic internal and external building patrols?

☐ Are student patrols used to augment campus security?

☐ Where campuses are linked by pathways, can campus security be organized into bicycle patrols?

In reply to demands for a speedier response and the need to get closer to the community, York University, Toronto, established a Pro-Active Cycle Team in 1991 of four uniformed officers and one student. Bicycle patrols were found to have greater visibility than security personnel in automobiles, served as a deterrent, and generated a more positive response from campus users.

ACCESS TO BUILDINGS

☐ Is access to classroom and office buildings reduced after hours and on weekends by limiting access to one entrance and staffing it?

☐ Or by requiring an access code?

☐ In new buildings, is it possible to install a "smart card" system for residences and offices so that a computerized log is generated when a door is accessed?

☐ Do people working late at night or overnight have access to a telephone or a cellular phone?

☐ Has consideration been given to photo identification cards for all faculty, staff, and students?

☐ In scheduling night classes, is it possible to avoid scattering evening classes in remote buildings?

☐ When classes are held off campus, has a security assessment been done of off-campus space?

York University, Toronto, has established a pilot project where the Campus Security lends out cellular telephones to staff and students working late in science labs. The Faculty of Fine Arts is making cellular phones available to faculty and students working late. There are also demands from caretaking and maintenance staff for access to cellular telephones.

STUDENT RESIDENCES

☐ Are there locks on both exterior doors and individual rooms?

☐ Are there peepholes on all residence room doors?

☐ Are the locks or combinations changed regularly?

☐ Are there regular patrols of the buildings or surrounding grounds?

☐ Are telephones visible and readily accessible on each floor?

☐ Are residents educated in the dangers of propping residence or building doors open?

SEMIPUBLIC AREAS

☐ Are semipublic areas patrolled regularly?

☐ Are they secured when not in use?

☐ Is it possible to build smaller facilities, e.g., several campus pubs, rather than one large one that attracts hundreds of people?

Lounges, cafeterias, shopping malls, and pubs are areas that attract outsiders to the campus as well as being used by the university community. Many security incidents on campuses are alcohol related. Programs that curb excessive alcohol use on campus affect crime rates.

DESIGN AND DEVELOPMENT PROCESSES

☐ Are all drawings and designs for new buildings or renovations reviewed for their security implications?

☐ Are new buildings or renovations pre-wired to install intrusion alarms?

☐ Are sites for emergency telephones established in the preconstruction phase of a project?

☐ Are security staff and users with security concerns involved in university construction committees to comment on designs in initial phases?

☐ Has the university developed a design standard on security that can serve as a minimum requirement for tenders on campus projects?

☐ Has the university developed a model contract for contractors and subcontractors requiring attention to safe routes, the continuity of construction hoarding, and contract compliance around sexual harassment by contractors?

The University of Toronto requires that the Personal Safety Officer sign off on designs for all new buildings or retrofits of existing buildings. The university has developed a design standard for campus security and a new model contract for contractors and subcontractors addressing campus safety.

TRAINING OF CAMPUS SECURITY

☐ Is campus security staff trained in preventive patrols?

☐ Are staff members trained to respond appropriately to sexual harassment and sexual assault?

☐ Is security staff trained to be sensitive to crimes against women and to understand their root causes?

☐ Is campus security involved with other campus groups in crime prevention initiatives, including meetings with students during orientation?

☐ Is training provided in race relations?

☐ Is training in interpersonal communication and awareness of the culture and values of the university provided to staff?

COMMUNITY PARTICIPATION IN CAMPUS SECURITY

☐ Are there mechanisms for involving all segments of the campus community in safety concerns, e.g., through a security committee?

☐ Are campus safety audits of specific buildings or facilities designed and managed by immediate users of those spaces?

☐ Is information made available to parents, students, and employees of the university about the incidence of campus crimes?

The College of Architecture and Landscape Architecture at the University of Minnesota, Minneapolis–St. Paul, sponsored a student design competition to improve the safety of a pedestrian bridge linking the Minneapolis and St. Paul parts of the campus. The competition raised consciousness of the need to address design issues on campus safety by involving all sectors of the university community, including architecture students, campus security staff, and politicians at the local and state levels.

POLICIES ON SEXUAL ASSAULT AND HARASSMENT ON CAMPUS

☐ Are explicit policies in place on student conduct, emphasizing that rape, sexual harassment, and sexual assault will not be tolerated on campus?

☐ Is there an overall strategy in place to respond to sexual assaults and date rape?

☐ Are there education programs in place to teach prevention strategies?

☐ Are streetproofing workshops made available to the university community?

☐ Are there effective programs to assist victims of sexual assaults, such as medical treatment, referrals, and training of campus personnel, including campus security?

☐ Are there procedures to encourage victims to report sexual assaults?

COLLECTIVE AGREEMENTS

☐ Do collective agreements on campus cover security under conditions of employment?

Some unions have inserted "campus safety clauses" into their collective agreements with university employers. At York University, Toronto, the 1991–92 Collective Agreement between York University and the Canadian Union of Educational Workers, Local 3, states under clause 15.02.1 "Health and Safety" that "The Union and the Employer recognize the right of employees to work in a secure, healthy, and accessible environment with adequate lighting where needed, a prominent display of directional signs, wheelchair accessibility, clean air in working areas, public and emergency telephones, an efficient and safe escort service, and an adequate security service."

NOTES

1. B. M. Rutherford and G. R. Wekerle, "Captive rider, captive labor: spatial constraints and women's employment," *Urban Geography* 9, 2 (1988), 116–37.

2. GLC Women's Committee, *Women on the Move* (London: 1987).

3. MTA, "New Yorkers' Perceptions of Subway and Bus Service: A Tracking Study," (1989), 5.

4. MTA, *TA Market Segmentation Study* (N.Y.: 1989).

5. Project for Public Spaces, *Managing Downtown Public Spaces* (Washington, D.C.: Planners Press, 1984).

6. Nottingham Safer Cities Project, *Steering Group Report on Community Safety in the City Center* (Nottingham, U.K., 1990).

7. W. H. Whyte, *City: Rediscovering the Center* (New York: Anchor Doubleday, 1988).

8. S. Trench, T. Oc, and S. Tiesdell, University of Nottingham, "Safer cities for women—perceived risks and planning measures" (Association of Collegiate Schools of Planning, Oxford, England, 1991).

9. Home Office Crime Preventive Unit, *Safer Cities Progress Report, 1989–1990* (London: Home Office).

10. R. M. Titus, "Security works: shopping enclaves bring hope, investment to blighted inner-city neighborhoods," *Urban Land* (January 1990), 2–5.

11. M. Zwolinski, "Store license at stake in Parkdale drug fight," *Toronto Star* (June 11, 1993).

12. Editorial, "Curbing attacks on corner stores," *Toronto Star* (March 14, 1993).

13. R. M. Titus, *Urban Land*, 2–5.

14. Ibid.

15. O. Newman, *Defensible Space* (New York: Macmillan, 1972).

16. A. Coleman, *Utopia on Trial* (London: Hilary Shipman, 1985).

17. D. Chapin, "Making green spaces safer places, experiences in New York City," *Landscape Architectural Review* 12, 3 (July 1991), 16–18.

18. D. Orsini, *Mitigating Fear in the Landscape: Recommendations for Enhancing Users' Perceptions of Safety in Urban Parks* (Master of Landscape Architecture Paper, University of Guelph, 1990).

19. D. Orsini, "Natural areas: places of beauty and fear," *Toronto Field Naturalist* (May 1993), 13–14.

20. J. Burgess, C. M. Harrison, and M. Limb, "People, parks and the urban green: a study of popular meanings and values for open spaces in the city," *Urban Studies* 25 (1988), 455–73.

21. Burgess, Harrison, and Limb, *Urban Studies*, 455–73.

22. P. L. Brown, "Reclaiming a park for play," *New York Times* (September 12, 1993).

23. J. Belan, "Safety and security in High Park, Toronto: A case study," *Landscape Architectural Review* 12, 3 (1991), 19–21.

24. D. Chapin, *Landscape Architectural Review*, 16–18.

25. New York Times, "Park program puts homeless to work," *New York Times* (October 31, 1993).

26. We are grateful to David Orsini for detailed comments he made on an earlier draft of this section.

27. The lead article by A. Matthews, "The campus crime wave: The ivory tower becomes an armed camp," *New York Times Magazine* (March 7, 1993), 38 ff. illustrates how perceptions of campuses have shifted over the last few years.

28. B. Lott, M. E. Reilly, and D. R. Howard. "Sexual assault and harassment: A campus community case study," *Signs* 8 (1982), 296–319; N. Kirk, "Factors affecting perceptions of safety in a campus environment," ed. J. Sime *Safety in the Built Environment* (London: E. and F. Spon, 1988), 285–96.

5

The Economic Costs of Crime

Many city officials have not seen crime as an urgent threat to the overall community that must be given a high priority on the civic agenda. Perhaps city governments will be more motivated to act when they consider the economic costs of crime. The killings of nine tourists in a year in Florida focused public attention on the economic costs of crime to the Florida economy. Tourism is a $31 billion-a-year industry.[1] Tourism operators estimated that European bookings could drop off by 20 percent due to fear of violent crime. This represents a possible loss of $6 billion a year. If American tourists also begin to avoid Florida, the total loss could be much higher.

Media accounts of the Florida tourist shootings linked violent crime, fear of crime, and economic losses in a major industry. Other commentators pointed out that these linkages also apply to the phenomenon of white flight to the suburbs and the impoverishment of American inner cities. A *New York Times* editorial, headlined "A murderous double standard," commented "Affluent whites' lives are valuable; poor blacks' lives are not. That's one dismal conclusion when a country accepts wholesale slaughter in ghetto streets, then gets outraged over the murders of three foreign tourists in Florida."[2] Of 1191 murders in Florida last year, 22 victims were from outside the state.

The Florida tourist murders show that the prospect of losing billions of dollars from the state economy has galvanized a response to violent crime that decades of increasing lawlessness did not accomplish.

Less dramatically, the fear of financial losses through successful civil suits brought by individuals has also elicited a response from institutions and property owners. Crime victims are demanding compensation for crime-related losses and injuries in civil courts. They are suing third parties, including hotel owners, universities and schools, and landlords of commercial and residential buildings, for failing to take sufficient security precautions to prevent criminal attacks on their premises, particularly if the risk of criminal attack was reasonably foreseeable. Where poor building design can be linked to the criminal attack, engineers, architects, planners, and other professionals may also be named as defendants.

Third parties may be held responsible for damages for the criminal acts of others in two ways:[3] when the third party stands in a relationship of duty to the victim or when the third party has a legal obligation to act. A duty to protect from the criminal acts of third persons can arise in several situations. In common law, common carriers have a duty to protect passengers from the foreseeable criminal acts of third persons. This duty extends beyond the trip itself to the paths that take a person to a place of safety. Thus common carriers have been held liable when passengers are left at unsafe locations. Innkeepers are required to take actions to protect guests from the foreseeable acts of third parties. This also extends to colleges and universities and places of public accommodation or usage. In all these cases, litigation has been based on the principle that crimes may be encouraged by the failure to protect against a known and identifiable risk of harm.

There is evidence that both the number of third party premises liability lawsuits and the size of the awards has increased substantially. Between 1978 and 1987, one study found that the average judgment increased from under $100,000 to more than $800,000.[4] Civil suits against landlords have been brought as negligence actions. In cases where tenants have been raped because adequate locks were not provided on doors, landlords have been charged with negligent failure to provide adequate security, negligent maintenance of the building, and a breach of contract (the rental agreement) to provide secure housing. In one of the most widely publicized cases, Connie Francis (Garzilli v. Howard Johnson Motor Lodges Inc., D.C.N.Y. 1976) was awarded a settlement of $1,800,000. Francis was sexually assaulted by a man who came through the sliding glass door to her motel room, a door that could be easily unlocked from the outside. In another case, Feld v. Merriam (Philadelphia County C.P. Ct., Pa. Jan. 1980), a woman tenant and her husband were awarded $6,000,000 against the apartment complex owners when three armed men assaulted them in the parking garage of the high-rise complex in which they lived. Both the tenants' association and a security company had warned the landlord several times that security was inadequate, but nothing was done. Perhaps the largest settlement, $17 million, was awarded in 1991 to Juli Bliskey against her apartment landlord in Corpus Christi, Texas. She was raped by an assailant who broke into the management office and obtained building keys to the apartment of young single women tenants.[5] Negligent failure to provide adequate security and reckless indifference were cited in making the award of damages.[6] Civil suits have also found landlords in breach of the covenant of quiet enjoyment and in breach of the warranty of habitability when residents have been violently attacked on the premises. Where there were prior attacks on the premises, landlords have been found guilty of negligent breach of duty to protect tenants against foreseeable attacks.[7]

In September 1992, Title II of the Student Right to Know Campus Security Act (1990) required U.S. colleges and universities to document and report annual campus crime statistics if they received federal funds. When institutions fail to inform students or staff of potentially dangerous situations, they leave themselves open to civil suits from victims of campus crimes or their families. Civil suits against universities and colleges have often involved inadequate building security. In Mullins v. Pine Manor College, $400,000 was awarded to a student who was raped on the grounds that the college did not take reasonable precautions to provide a secure living environment.[8] In addition, campus officials were found personally liable for failing to take reasonable precautions to prevent foreseeable crimes. In another case, Siciliano v. State of California (San Francisco County Super. Ct., Cal. Jan. 28, 1981), a female attorney was sexually assaulted in the law school rest room. She was awarded $210,000 on the grounds that the university had shown a negligent failure to provide adequate security; the lack of security constituted a dangerous condition of public property. In Peterson v. the San Francisco Community College District, the college was held liable for failing to trim overgrown shrubbery adjacent to the stairway of a campus parking lot where a female student was attacked in daylight, after other attacks had occurred at that location. The college had failed to trim the shrubbery or warn students of the risk.[9]

Public authorities have also been held liable for negligent security in civil courts. In Wesley v. Greyhound Lines Inc. (Wake County Sup. Ct., N.C., 1977), a woman customer using the bus depot was sexually assaulted at knifepoint in the women's room lounge. The bus station had been newly built, with little consideration given to urban safety in the design. There had also been a history of crimes at the depot. The woman was awarded $150,000 of compensatory damages on the grounds that the bus company was guilty of negligent security and that a public carrier's high standard of care also applies to the bus depot. In the case of Gordon v. Chicago Transit Authority (Illinois, Cook County Superior Court, 1983) a woman was awarded $200,000 after she was raped at a transit station. The court ruled that the transit authority had a duty to provide security guards despite the presence of police in the area.[10] In a more recent case in San Francisco, a woman who had sought refuge on a bus from an attacker was ordered off the bus by the bus driver who did not want to get involved. After she was dragged away and raped by her assailant, she successfully sued the city and was awarded $1.6 million.[11]

The more foreseeable the crime, the greater the duty to provide security.[12] With a new focus on facility design as a deterrent to site specific crimes, architects and other design practitioners are also being sued. Within the design professions, the standard of care owed clients is being redefined to include the obligation to design facilities that reduce rather than enhance opportunities for crime. Practitioners who neglect to include design for urban safety in new or retrofitted facilities leave themselves open to litigation. There is a responsibility to take steps to prevent attacks if such attacks are foreseeable. Otherwise, design practitioners and planners may be liable for negligence and assessed damages. In practice, this means that architects, for example, must assess the risks of criminal activity associated with their buildings that might be attributable to design, to a specific site, or location in a specific neighborhood that is a crime magnet. A property must be at least as well protected as its neighbor, since the least protected property in an area will be the easier target. There is also a responsibility to educate clients so that building owners are willing to pay for crime prevention measures and to maintain them over time.

The growth in third party premises liability suits may raise overall safety standards in the long run. They empower the victims of crime and give landlords a powerful incentive to take measures to try to prevent crime from occurring. Business owners, landlords, and public service providers have a financial incentive to make crime prevention a priority in the initial design and planning of the built environment and to allocate funds for ongoing security. Increasingly, business owners are conducting their own vulnerability and threat analysis to become better aware of the nature and frequency of crimes committed in the general vicinity, among similar businesses, and in their own business. They have a duty to be aware of crime trends and to respond in an appropriate manner. This gives business owners and public sector service providers a real stake in monitoring crime trends in neighborhoods and specific urban locales as well as paying particular attention to crime patterns in their own businesses. It gives them common cause with community groups and public bodies in identifying the causes of crime and developing localized responses. Measured against the potential of large financial settlements to the victims of crime, the costs of crime prevention through design and community-based solutions begin to make real economic and social sense.

In a society that often measures value in monetary terms, the trend to estimate the financial impacts of crime on victims and on cities may provide a powerful incentive to act proactively and affirmatively. However, there is the real danger that security precautions will take the form of target hardening and fortress building, isolating people within secure enclaves while lawlessness rages outside the protected boundaries.

This book has focused on the myriad small grass roots initiatives that can prevent not only crime but also contribute to the development of community. We have emphasized strategies of social prevention as well as changes to physical design, on the assumption that the two approaches work together and cannot be separated. We have argued that changes in the built environment are often a starting point to responding to crime and fear of crime. Concrete changes to our living and work environments and to urban public space are immediately felt and provide an opportunity to engage users of these places in making change. But making cities safer cannot be limited to design changes. Urban crime is deeply rooted in cultural practices and systems of privilege and disadvantage that are ordered by gender, class, and race. Improving urban safety cannot be divorced from eliminating violence against women, reducing poverty and racism, and creating cities that are more equitable and just.

NOTES

1. L. Diebel, "Killings put chill on tourism in Sunshine State," *Toronto Star* (September 19, 1993); "Florida shootings underline economic cost of crime," *Toronto Star* (from editorial in *Baltimore Sun*) (September 20, 1993).

2. Editorial, "A murderous double standard," *New York Times* (September 23, 1993).

3. S. E. Loggans, "Rape as intentional tort: first and third party liability," *Trial* 20, 10 (October 1985), 45–48.

4. D. B. Kennedy, "Architectural concerns regarding security and premises liability," *Journal of Architectural and Planning Research* 10, 2 (Summer 1993), 105–29.

5. "Rape victims sue over safety," *American Bar Association Journal* 77 (December 1991), 34–35.

6. Institute for the Study of Sexual Assault, *Civil Sexual Assault Cases: Judgements and Settlements* (San Francisco: Institute for the Study of Sexual Assault, 1983, 1985, 1987).

7. Institute for the Study of Sexual Assault, 1983, 1985, 1987.

8. M. Grannis, J. L. Nasar, and B. Fisher, "Proximate physical cues to fear of crime," paper presented at Association of Collegiate Schools of Planning Conference, Columbus, Ohio, 1992. Paper available from M. Grannis, The Ohio State University.

9. Grannis, Nasar, and Fisher, "Proximate physical cues . . . ," 1992.

10. Institute for the Study of Sexual Assault, 1983, 1985, 1987.

11. Associated Press, "Rape victim gets $1.6 million after being ordered off bus," *Toronto Star* (July 15, 1993).

12. An excellent overview and critique of these issues is provided by D. B. Kennedy, "Architectural concerns regarding security and premises liability," *Journal of Architectural and Planning Research* 10, 2 (Summer, 1993), 105–29. The following paragraph provides a summary of arguments from this paper.

APPENDICES

Appendix 1

METRAC Safety Audit Guide

INTRODUCTION

Our society's tolerance of violence against women has been with us for a long time, and old ways of doing things are hard to change. But society—thanks to the hard work and determination of thousands of women—has already begun to make changes.

Over the last ten years, countless stories have taught us how often violence against women happens in our communities. What used to be seen as private—between two people—has become a public and social issue. Governments and public services such as universities and transportation companies are taking more responsibility for women's safety.

From working with women in many places over the years, it's clear to us at METRAC that women know a lot that traditional experts don't know about the environment and how its design affects how safe women feel.

It's still true that architects, urban planners, and the police are usually men. They may not mean to, but they often don't understand what it's like to be a woman alone, late at night, waiting for a bus, walking to her car in an isolated parking lot, or walking home along a dark path.

In conducting a safety audit, women are the experts. It's women's experience with places that counts.

We hope METRAC's guide on how to conduct safety audits answers the questions you have, and that it inspires you to work to change the places in your community where you feel unsafe or uncomfortable.

What is a safety audit?

The basic idea of a safety audit is to look at a place that bothers you and note problems: What's the lighting like? Would anyone hear you if you called for help? What improvements would you like to see?

It sounds simple and it is. You don't have to have a degree in architecture or urban planning to conduct a safety audit. Living as a woman has given each of us a lifetime of experience and knowledge about what works and what doesn't work—about where we feel comfortable and where we don't.

The main goal of the safety audit is to reduce the opportunity for sexual assaults or harassment. A place that discourages sexual assault will also lower the chance of other crimes.

Safety audits are concrete and practical. They are part of changing the world to make it safer for women and better for everyone. METRAC has used the women's safety audit method successfully with:

- the Toronto Transit Commission (TTC) in every subway station
- city planners to audit High Park (Toronto's largest park)
- university staff and students to audit campuses
- other cities and towns in Ontario

The women's safety audit guide has been used by women across Canada and in other parts of the world.

The focus of this guide is women's safety, but an audit can also help you with other safety concerns in your community. For example, a place that women feel safe in is a safer place for children, people who are mentally challenged, and older people. It is a place less likely to hide muggers and drug traffickers. If places are safer for women, they are safer for everyone.

The rest of this book will outline the steps you need to follow to do your own safety audit. The five main sections show you:

1. how to invite others to join you
2. how to prepare for an audit
3. how to conduct an audit
4. what you need to do after you've finished the audit
5. some ideas for special types of audits

1. TALKING TO OTHERS

Audits don't have to involve a lot of people. But often the very places you want to audit are those where you feel unsafe, and the best time to audit is at night, so we recommend that you conduct the audit with other people.

You can start by talking to people or groups you know. For example, you could contact:

- friends and neighbors
- a tenants' or residents' association
- your church group or a women's group

If you are conducting the audit at work, invite women you work with and your union or staff representative.

If you are auditing your university or college campus, invite student union members, the women's center, and the staff.[1]

Inviting others to come on the safety audit

You may want to invite people to join you on the audit who can help you get improvements made, such as your city councillor or school trustee, reporters from a community newspaper, or the person in charge of a place that concerns you.

2. DEFINING THE AUDIT

How big an area do you want to cover?

Sometimes it's not clear how big an area you want to audit—one building, a street, a neighborhood, or the entire city. You may want to start small. For example, if your concern is the whole neighborhood, you could:

- conduct a full audit of a typical street
- audit the whole neighborhood from the point of view of one or two factors such as lighting and signs
- audit your route to and from the bus stop, the store, or the community center

At work or school, you may want to look at the places that most concern you. These may be washrooms, parking lots, stairways, tunnels, or any isolated areas.

A survey handed out, in advance, around the neighborhood or in the building is one way to find out where women in the area feel most unsafe or uncomfortable.

Survey questions could include:

1. How safe do you feel in your building/on the street/waiting at the bus stop?
2. Have you limited what you do because you don't feel safe?
3. Have you ever felt unsafe, or at risk of sexual assault in this area?
4. Please list five specific places where you feel most unsafe.
5. Please comment on what would help you to feel safer.

Audits have been conducted in different ways. For example:

- The cities of Kitchener–Waterloo invited women to participate; in one night they conducted an audit of the areas in the city that bothered them most.
- Over a five-month period, every building and outdoor area on campus was audited at Queen's University.
- A neighborhood group encouraged residents to conduct audits on their own street and to hand in the results to the residents' association.

- Employees in an office building audited their workplace, the parking garage, and bus stops in both the summer and winter.

How many people should be on an audit team?

The best size for an audit team is three to seven people. This size allows for different points of view, but is still small enough to have lots of discussion. If you want to cover a large space such as a neighborhood, you will need more than one team.

The audit group

The audit group should reflect the needs of women in the whole community. If this isn't possible, try to be aware of the points of view of other women who might be:

- using a wheelchair
- hard of hearing
- blind
- mentally challenged
- very young
- elderly
- poor
- lesbians
- shift workers
- traveling with young children
- carrying parcels
- members of a minority culture
- unable to read
- not familiar with English

Time frame

The ideal time to allow for a "first audit" seems to be approximately two to three hours. You will need about one-half to one hour to talk about the audit and decide on the location and size, one to one and a half hours to conduct the audit, one-half to one hour to discuss the findings and plan to write the recommendations. If the same group is continuing to work together, you may not need as much time for other audits.

3. CONDUCTING AN AUDIT

What you need for the audit

- Take a flashlight along.
- Your notes will photocopy better if you use a red or black pen or marker instead of a blue one.

- Take a camera, if you have one. If you're going out at night, use a high-speed film—not less than 400 ASA (high-speed films can be used to take pictures indoors). It's also a good idea to write down the number of each photo and where it was taken.
- Take notes or use your camera to document *positive* features as well as problem areas. It can be very powerful to be able to contrast good and bad examples of the same factor—for example, a well-lit street and a poorly lit street.
- If it's difficult for you to take notes, use a tape recorder.
- It is important to talk to women you meet during the audit. Introduce yourself. Tell them that you are looking at women's safety in the area and would like to know what they think. You might ask how often and why they are there, whether they have ever had any bad experiences, and what changes they'd like to see.
- Remember to dress appropriately and to go to the washroom before you go out. (It's amazing what a difference this one makes.)
- Ensure each participant has safe transportation home from the audit.

When to audit

- Time of Day

METRAC recommends conducting audits after dark, especially outside audits. It's the only way to know if there is a problem with lighting—one of the most important safety features. Nighttime is also the time of day when women are most isolated and feel least safe.

Many women avoid going out alone at night. They don't want the anxiety or the risk. It's unfair, and we know many women share METRAC's goal of making our cities safe for women 24 hours a day.

But sometimes a place is more deserted and scary early in the morning, or in the middle of the afternoon when everyone else is away at work. Only you will know which part of each 24 hours is of most concern *to you*.

- Time of Year

Seasons also affect how safe the place feels. Safety concerns are different when tree branches and bushes are bare in winter than when trees and plants are in full bloom in summer and might hide an attacker or block out light. Dry parking lots are different from when they are full of puddles, covered in ice, or surrounded by snowbanks that block the view.

You may want to go back to the same place more than once to see what it's like at different times of day, week, or year. You can also check up on how well or poorly the place is maintained.

Using a checklist

You've decided to conduct an audit because you don't feel safe in part of the city and you want to do something about it. The idea, then, is to gather the information that will help you press for changes.

The questions you're trying to answer are:

- Why don't I like this place?
- When and why do I feel uncomfortable here?
- What changes would make me feel safer?

In METRAC's experience, taking the time to think about the factors on a checklist helps to see places better.

Stopping to look closely at different factors also lets people share feelings about a place. Sometimes one person will remember something, and that will bring out another story. Each of these stories helps determine why a place does or doesn't feel comfortable.

Finally, if you are working with other people who don't understand the problems as well as you, the checklist can help you work together. Your superintendent may want to rush past an area, but the checklist can help you to say "Hey, wait a minute. We need to look at the lighting here before we move on."

When you look at a space, think about how you use it:

- What if you were walking alone here late at night?
- What if you had to wait for someone to come and pick you up?
- Is this doorway a possible entrapment site?
- Does it feel safe in winter? in the rain?
- Are there fewer people around at different times of the day, week, or year?

Going through a checklist takes the whole picture and breaks it down into parts.

** You can photocopy and enlarge the
checklist on the following pages to make
it bigger and easier to write on **

SAFETY AUDIT CHECKLIST

☐ OUTDOOORS   ☐ INDOORS

GENERAL AREA: _____

SPECIFIC LOCATION: _____

DATE: _____ DAY: _____ TIME: _____

AUDITED BY: _____

REASON FOR AUDITING THE AREA:

_____

1. General Impressions

Your gut reactions: _____

What 5 words best describe the place?

_____

2. Lighting

Impression of lighting: ☐ very poor   ☐ poor   ☐ satisfactory   ☐ good
       ☐ very good   ☐ too dark   ☐ too bright
Is the lighting even?   ☐ yes   ☐ no
How many lights are out? _____
What proportion of lights are out? _____

(e.g., Maybe only two bulbs in your hallway are burned out, but if there are only three bulbs to start with, then a more powerful way to say this is that two-thirds of the lights are out.)

Are you able to identify a face 25 yards away?   ☐ yes   ☐ no
Do you know where/whom to call if lights are out, broken, not yet turned on, etc.?
         ☐ yes   ☐ no
Outdoors: Is the lighting obscured by trees or bushes?   ☐ yes   ☐ no
How well does the lighting illuminate pedestrian walkways and sidewalks?
       ☐ very poorly   ☐ poorly   ☐ satisfactorily   ☐ well   ☐ very well
How clearly does the lighting illuminate directional signs or maps?
       ☐ very poorly   ☐ poorly   ☐ satisfactorily   ☐ well   ☐ very well

3. Signage

Is there a sign (i.e., room no., building name) identifying where you are?
         ☐ yes   ☐ no
If no, are there directional signs or maps nearby that can help you identify where you are?
         ☐ yes   ☐ no
Are there signs that show you where to get emergency assistance if needed?
         ☐ yes   ☐ no
Are there signs that direct you to wheelchair access?   ☐ yes   ☐ no

Do exit doors identify where they exit to? ☐ yes ☐ no
Is there information posted describing the hours the building is legitimately open?
☐ yes ☐ no

Impression of overall signage: ☐ very poor ☐ poor ☐ satisfactory
☐ good ☐ very good

What signs should be added?

4. Sightlines

Can you clearly see what's up ahead? ☐ yes ☐ no
If no, why not?
Indoors: ☐ sharp corners ☐ walls ☐ pillars
Outdoors: ☐ bushes ☐ fences ☐ hill

☐ other _____
Are there places someone could be hiding? ☐ yes ☐ no

If yes, where?

What would make it easier to see?
E.g.: ☐ transparent materials such as glass
☐ angled corners ☐ security mirrors
☐ trimmed bushes ☐ snow cleared
☐ vehicles moved
Other comments? _____

_____

_____

_____

5. Isolation—Eye Distance

At the time of your audit, does the area feel isolated? ☐ yes ☐ no
How many people are likely to be around?
● *In the early morning:*
☐ none ☐ a few ☐ several ☐ many
● *During the day:*
☐ none ☐ a few ☐ several ☐ many
● *In the evening:*
☐ none ☐ a few ☐ several ☐ many
● *Late at night (after 10 P.M.):*
☐ none ☐ a few ☐ several ☐ many
Is it easy to predict when people will be around? ☐ yes ☐ no
Is there a monitor or surveillance system? ☐ yes ☐ no ☐ don't know

Other comments? _____

_____

_____

_____

6. Isolation—Ear Distance

How far away is the nearest person to hear a call for help? _____
☐ don't know

How far away is the nearest emergency service such as an alarm, security personnel, crisis telephone? _____ ☐ don't know

Can you see a telephone or a sign directing you to emergency assistance?
☐ yes ☐ no

Is the area patrolled? ☐ yes ☐ no ☐ don't know

If yes, how frequently? ☐ every hour ☐ once per afternoon/evening
☐ don't know

Other comments? _____

_____

_____

_____

7. Movement Predictors (a predictable or unchangeable route or path)

How easy is it to predict a woman's movements (e.g., her route)?
☐ very easy ☐ somewhat obvious ☐ no way of knowing

Is there an alternative well-lit and frequently traveled route or path available?
☐ yes ☐ no ☐ don't know

Can you tell what is at the other end of the path, tunnel, or walkway?
☐ yes ☐ no

Are there corners, alcoves, or bushes where someone could hide and wait for you?
☐ yes ☐ no

Other comments? _____

_____

_____

_____

8. Possible Entrapment Sites

Indoors:

Are there empty rooms that should be locked? ☐ yes ☐ no

Are there small, well-defined areas?

e.g.: ☐ stairwells ☐ recessed doorways or lockers
☐ elevators ☐ unlocked closets

Outdoors:

Are there small, confined areas where you would be hidden from view?

e.g.: ☐ between garbage bins ☐ unlocked equipment or utility shed
☐ alley or laneway ☐ recessed doorway ☐ construction site

Other: _____

9. Escape Routes

How easy would it be for an offender to disappear?
   ☐ very easy   ☐ quite easy   ☐ not very easy
Is there more than one exit?   ☐ yes   ☐ no   ☐ don't know

10. Nearby Land Uses

What is the surrounding or nearby land used for?
   ☐ stores   ☐ offices   ☐ restaurants   ☐ factories   ☐ residential
   houses and streets   ☐ busy traffic   ☐ heavily treed/wooded area
   ☐ riverbank   ☐ parking lots   ☐ campus buildings   ☐ don't know

   Other: _____
Can you identify who owns or maintains nearby land?   ☐ yes   ☐ no
Impressions of nearby land use:
   ☐ very poor   ☐ poor   ☐ satisfactory   ☐ good   ☐ very good

11. Maintenance

Impressions of maintenance: ☐ very poor   ☐ poor   ☐ satisfactory
                                            ☐ good   ☐ very good
Is there litter lying around?   ☐ yes   ☐ no
Do you know to whom maintenance concerns should be reported?   ☐ yes   ☐ no
From your experience, how long do repairs generally take?
                     ☐ 1 day   ☐ within 1 week   ☐ 1–3 weeks
                     ☐ more than 3 weeks   ☐ don't know

12. Factors That Make the Place More Human

Does the place feel cared for?   ☐ yes   ☐ no
Does the place feel abandoned?   ☐ yes   ☐ no

   Why? _____

_____

Is there graffiti on the walls?   ☐ yes   ☐ no
In your opinion are there racist or sexist slogans/signs/images on the walls?
                                                           ☐ yes   ☐ no
Are there signs of vandalism?   ☐ yes   ☐ no
Would other materials, tones, textures, or colors improve your sense of safety?
                                                           ☐ yes   ☐ no

Other comments? _____

_____

_____

_____

_____

13. Overall Design

Impressions of overall design: ☐ very poor ☐ poor ☐ satisfactory
☐ good ☐ very good

If you weren't familiar with the place, would it be easy to find your way around?

☐ yes ☐ no

Does the place "make sense?" ☐ yes ☐ no
Is the place too spread out? ☐ yes ☐ no
Are there a confusing number of levels? ☐ yes ☐ no

Other comments? _____

_____

_____

_____

14. Improvements

What improvements would you like to see?

Do you have any specific recommendations?

Please send any in-progress or completed documentation or reports to:

METRAC, 158 Spadina Road, Toronto, Ontario, Canada M5R 2T8
(416) 392-3135   FAX (416) 392-3136

Tips on taking notes

- No matter how good your memory is, you won't remember everything, so it's important to take good notes. You may need to add some items and may not need others, but our experience is that using a checklist and writing notes on it will make it easier to organize your ideas and suggestions later on.
- Write down any questions that you have (even if you don't have the time to find the answers).
- Sometimes a place is so poorly designed that there aren't any real solutions, only bandaid ones. But it is still important to note that there's a problem. Identifying and naming a problem is the beginning of changing the way new buildings and spaces are designed.
- Take notes on everything, including your comments on the process of the audit itself.
- Look over your notes a day or two later to see if they still make sense. Would

someone who wasn't on the audit understand what you mean? If not, try to make your notes clearer.

4. AFTER THE AUDIT

Organizing your findings

After you've conducted the audit, you'll have a lot of information about problem areas, and a lot of ideas about changes you'd like to see.

One way of organizing the information is to group together all the points on one factor such as "lighting." Comments about how far a woman has to go to get help, whether there are enough telephones nearby, and how likely it is that other people might see an assault can be brought together under "isolation" factors.

Another way of organizing the information from the checklist(s) is by type of space. For example, safety factors common to all parking lots would be grouped together.

When you've finished organizing the findings, you should check to see if any part of the area has been overlooked. If it has, consider collecting more information with a mini-audit, or by asking people in the area.

Sharing the results

Whether they were part of the audit or not, you might want to get support, information, ideas, and feedback from people living or working in the area. If there are people who couldn't come on the audit, now is the time to include them. Consider holding small meetings where those who did not participate can talk about their concerns and help with the recommendations. This way, you'll know more about the problems, get ideas about what could be done, and get support for the changes you want to see.

Making recommendations

Your **first** step is to look at the checklist(s) and decide what the most important concerns are. The **second** step is to make recommendations that solve the problems. For example, if the audit shows that buildings are hard to identify and find, then the recommendation might be to put up signs. Signs need to be readable at night and by those who may be blind (for example, lit signs with symbols instead of words, and braille signs).

Working for change

• Find out who is responsible.

If you're not sure who is responsible for the place, a good person to talk to is your town or city councillor. Call, write a letter, or ask for a meeting. It is her or his responsibility to help you. She or he should also be able to tell you who owns what land and how to contact them, or who is responsible for what alley, street, or parking lot.

Call City Hall to speak to your municipal representatives, and if they aren't helpful, you can always go directly to the mayor.

- Get in touch with the people who are responsible.

Call them or write them about the audit. Tell them about the problems you've found. Tell them what they have to do to make it better. And ask them to tell you what they will do about the problems, your suggestions, and how soon. (This is where it may help to have other women and other organizations to back you up.)

- Please contact METRAC.

Please send METRAC a copy of reports from safety audits you do and also any letters you send or receive. The more information we have about the places in cities that don't work for women, the better we are able to keep up the pressure for improvements to urban design and policy-making. You can write to us at 158 Spadina Road, Toronto, Ontario, Canada M5R 2T8; call us at (416) 392–3135 or fax information to (416) 392–3136.

Safety audits are a new idea. They are part of a process of change, so don't be surprised if you meet resistance to your suggestions. Here are some ideas you can use to respond:

- "It's not my department."

If the people you are talking to tell you that the issues you're raising are not their concern, ask them to tell you who *is* responsible. They may be right, or they may be avoiding something. Either way, they will at least be more aware of your concerns.

- Keep a diary of the people you contact.

It's a good idea to write down the names, titles, and phone numbers of the people you talk to, the dates of your calls, and what was said. It may be that no one will admit to being responsible, and that you are sent in circles. In these cases, you will be in a good position to pressure for a better response if you can show all the effort that has gone into trying to get basic changes made to improve women's safety.

- Try other people.

If writing or talking to politicians gets you nowhere, try their staff. If the staff is the problem, try the politicians directly. If owners want nothing to do with you, call the politicians, or their staff, or the media.

- Keep the pressure on.

Once someone has agreed to make improvements, get them to write you a letter. Ask them to say when the changes will be made. If they don't keep their promises, continue to write or call, and get other people to write or call too.

- Beware of the "Perception vs Reality" debate.

Sometimes the people who are responsible for a space will try to tell you that the place only seems unsafe, but that "in reality" it is safe, that nothing has ever happened there. This response denies the *reality* of women's experiences. If a woman feels uncomfortable enough about a space to go to the trouble of doing an audit, there *is* a problem. Tell them that you know there is a problem and don't accept their argument.

> *Women's safety concerns have not been*
> *considered important. It's time to put*
> *them at the top of the priority list.*

5. SPECIAL AUDITS

Large audits

If you want to conduct an audit of a city, or another large area, you will need to do a lot of extra planning. We can't tell you everything you'll need to do, but here are some things to think about:

- How many teams do you need?
- Do you have maps and any other important information?
- Can you arrange for safe transportation to and from the audit areas? What about child care?
- How will you organize the volunteers, train the team leaders, collect the check-lists, write a summary report and recommendations?
- How will you present the findings?

If the place being audited is large or complex, then the audit and notes should focus on one part at a time. For example, when METRAC was auditing Toronto's subway system, 3 to 15 copies of the checklist were filled in for each subway station, depending on its size and complexity. One checklist might be only the station platform, another the tunnel, one for the passenger pickup area, etc.—any area where lighting, availability of help, and other factors were considered.

Joint audits

If there are a lot of safety problems in your area (or you want to do a large area), and if you have a lot of energy, you could press for a joint audit team before you go out on the audit.

When METRAC audited the subway system, we worked together with the Toronto Transit Commission and the Metro Police. It takes more time and effort at the beginning to get institutions such as these to be full partners in the audit. It also takes more time to work out how the audit is to be done. But then, having agreed to participate, they are more likely to take the actions needed to help solve problems.

Here is a list of some of the people you may wish to contact to be partners in a joint audit:

—sexual assault crisis centers
—neighborhood businesses (shops, restaurants, gas stations, 24-hour stores)
—residents associations
—transit representatives
—police
—elected representatives
—school representatives

Auditing the transit system

Whenever you are conducting an audit of a street area that includes a bus or streetcar stop, or a subway station, be sure to look carefully at where people wait for a bus, and how they get to and from the stops.

Here are some extra questions for auditing the transit system:

• How good is the lighting inside the shelter or subway station?
• How far away is the nearest public phone? the nearest private phone (commercial or residential)?
• Is there information visible for passengers about what to do in an emergency?

Auditing policies, practices, and services

It is important to remember that improving physical spaces is only one piece of a complex puzzle. Women's safety is affected not only by whether there are enough lights, emergency services such as telephones, or the number of other people around, but also by factors such as policies, practices, and services. And you can "audit" human and policy practices.

For example, at work, school, in the groups you belong to, in your housing complex, etc.:

• Do you trust the people you would have to go to for help if you have been sexually assaulted?
• Would they be sensitive to your needs?
• Do you have the information that you need about sexual assaults that have happened in your neighborhood or workplace?
• Do you have a say in decisions that affect your safety?

Here are some sample questions about policies and procedures—they can be adjusted to use in a housing project, a school, a community center, or a university:

1) Are there policies on sexual harassment?
   ☐ yes   ☐ no   ☐ don't know

   In your opinion, how well do they work?
   ☐ poor   ☐ satisfactory   ☐ good   ☐ very good

   Comment: _____

   _____

   _____

2) Do you know of any attacks or harassment of immigrants or people of color (racism)?
   ☐ yes   ☐ no   ☐ don't know
   What was the response?

   Comment: _____

   _____

3) Do you know of any incidents of harassment of, inappropriate touching of, or violence against women or children (sexism or sexual assault)?
   ☐ yes   ☐ no   ☐ don't know
   What was the response?

   Comment: _____

   _____

4) Do you know of any attacks or harassment of lesbians or gays (homophobia)?
   ☐ yes   ☐ no   ☐ don't know
   What was the response?

   Comment: _____

   _____

5) Are self-defense courses like the Wen-do model of awareness, avoidance, and action offered nearby?
   ☐ yes   ☐ no   ☐ don't know
   Is there a fee to take them?
   ☐ yes   ☐ no   ☐ don't know
   In your opinion, how well do they work?
   ☐ poor   ☐ satisfactory   ☐ good   ☐ very good

   Comment: _____

NOTES

1. METRAC has written a *Campus Safety Audit Guide* to look at the problems that are unique to campuses.

Appendix 2

Blake/Boultbee Women's Group/ Toronto Safety Audit Fall 1992

Written by: Darlene Sampson, Joyce Walsh, and Michelle Coutu

In Fall 1992, our Women's Group took a tour of the neighborhood for the purpose of conducting a safety audit. This group consists of ten women who are concerned about their surrounding neighborhood, neighbors, children, and ourselves. Blake/Boultbee consists of two apartment buildings and town houses; in between these buildings are walkways and crevices that are or could be very dangerous for members of the community.

10 BOULTBEE AVENUE

1. Underground garage

As we entered the underground garage through the elevator many women expressed apprehension. "There's a *very bad odor* . . . and it's very creepy." The group felt that the underground garage is isolated and has many entrapment sites. There is no one to scream to (the exhaust fan was loud), and there is no phone close by in order to get help if the need should ever arise. The pillars pose a safety problem. One of our members hid behind a pillar and no one in the group could tell where she was. On the pillars and walls we found no "exit" or "elevator" signs except for a small sign by the exit door. As we left the east side door, it locked behind us. We had to go up three flights of stairs and two closed doors and when we finally got to the lobby entrance there had been no signs indicating to us that this was the way to the lobby (only those who lived here know where to go).

"Two doors with no signs. Another flight of stairs not telling you where it goes." "Yeah, that's the one that leads to the hallway to the lobby. The door doesn't have anything on it. It

Credit: Blake/Boultbee Women's Group.

doesn't even have what floor it is, the main floor, nothing." "And as soon as you go out this door locks."

We suggest the following to make the underground garage safer:

- an emergency phone or a surveillance mechanism
- mirrors on the pillars in order to see around corners
- bigger and brighter signs
- "exit" and signs on all exit doors indicating where they are leading to

This area, on the other hand, was very well lit, it was well kept, and had the proper fire extinguishers installed. Signs saying "Be alert, check your backseat, lock your car" were also well appreciated.

2. Abandoned second garage (outside ramp)

Much to our surprise, as we exited the underground garage, we found that the ramp goes to an abandoned second garage. Although we were a group of people, many of the women found it difficult to explore this area because of how unsafe it felt. There was very low lighting; graffiti (e.g., a large penis) on the walls; broken glass / garbage and rusting pipes; it is far removed from people and there are plenty of places to hide. Rumor in the community has it that children use it to play, and drug dealers to do business. During our examination, one women in our group recounted a story: ". . . a woman was screaming her head off from the abandoned underground. I ran up to the guard (MTHA security guard) who said 'Uh, they're probably just partying in there or something.' . . . and I mean this woman was really screaming." *Poor security response makes this area even more unsafe.*

Other comments from the group: "They could drag you down here. Who could hear you down here? If they were to knock you out and drag you down here . . ." "It's not kept up. It obviously looks abandoned. The lighting is very low."

We suggest that the whole area be sealed off or renovated to make more parking for tenants (which is badly needed). In the meantime, *immediately*, there has to be better lighting and lots of surveillance.

3. Garage ramp

As we left the 10 Boultbee garage, which is where the abandoned garage starts, we noticed a lot of places to hide. There are cement blocks approximately three feet high that someone could easily hide behind. Walking up the ramp we noticed that the trees in the garden were growing over the lighting.

We found it well kept, well lit, and painted bright colors.

4. Stairwell to Withrow Avenue

Going up these stairs it is very bushy on both sides with only one light which the trees block. When reaching the landing going on to Withrow Avenue it is very dark with trees on one side and a house on the other. We found the streetlight on the opposite side of the street to this landing is very dim.

We are suggesting garden lights be put in the bushes on either side of the stairs, and brighter and more lights on Withrow Avenue. It is also important that trees blocking lighting be trimmed frequently.

5. Tenant parking lot

We noticed that there was a fence running along the edge of the parking lot and a laneway that is only half finished. This laneway is very dark and makes for a good entrapment site. This parking lot is dark on both ends (east and west). People can hide, especially on the west end of the parking lot because of the trees. We also found it dark on the pathway going from the parking lot to the building. From 10 Boultbee to the parking lot you cannot make out someone's face or even hear them (due to a fan). We found that the most unsafe time is in the early morning and late at night due to security not being on-site during these hours. We also noted that there is a "handicapped" sign for parking spots that is small and covered by trees.

"Look if you're leaving your car here and you have to walk, that's dark." "Let's say you didn't live in 10 Boultbee. Who can park in here, only 10 Boultbee residents?"

"Yeah, and visitors." "Anybody, really." "Now, see what I'm saying? Say you had to walk this way, it's so dark, all in here . . . who's gonna see ya?" "And it's dark right where the pathway is going up to the building. There's no sign saying this is the walkway to the building." "The sign I just happened to notice on the pole, couldn't tell what it was." "There's a sign over there, now if you can see that, good luck to you." (laughter) "All along here is so dark."

We are suggesting the following in order to make this parking lot a safer place:

- brighter lighting
- regular trimming of trees
- garden lights
- finish the fencing
- a light to be installed on the island going to 10 Boultbee
- a large sign pointing to 10 Boultbee and the security office

We feel that the parking lot was well kept, the security office is close by, and there was no graffiti.

BOULTBEE STREET

6. Town houses

As we came from the 10 Boultbee parking lot going down Boultbee Avenue by the town houses, we found that the lighting was low alongside the street and parking lot. There are bushes (shoulder height) in front of these town houses, behind which we found someone could hide quite easily. We also found broken glass. On the other side of this street is Blake School. We found that there were few lights and it was very dark. In fact, on the east side of the school is a big yard that is in total darkness.

"Do you feel someone could grab you and drag you back there with no lighting?" "Oh yeah, why not? Look at the field! Even if someone had you in the field. Look at that! You can't see anything!" "Nothing." "You can't see anything in the field."

We are suggesting the following:

- brighter lights
- lights installed on the school side
- a light to be installed in the yard on the east side of the school
- bushes be at least trimmed to a lesser height or replaced with something that provides safety and privacy but still looks good

As we walked along this street, we felt pretty safe due to the fact that there was more traffic and snoopy neighbors (people were checking out what we were doing from their windows). We felt that the porch lights being on an automatic timer is great. The corner town houses had bright spotlights at the top which makes the street corners brighter and safer. This street is also very well kept.

7. Archway/parkette

On our tour we came across a small park behind the town houses on Boultbee Avenue. This archway has no signs as to where it leads, and is covered by graffiti (but is very well lit). Once through this archway, you are surrounded by trees and darkness. It is a great hiding spot for prowlers, drug dealers, and any such characters. We noticed that there are also lights on top of these town houses which are being blocked by trees because of their height and width. Women commented: ". . . broken bottles in here all the time." In this area is a park that is surrounded by wood borders which anyone could easily fall over. While in this area you feel "helpless." "There's too many places where people can hide." "Let's get out of here." "I won't let my kids play back here."

Generally, the women felt that this parkette area is highly unsafe. All women in the group said that they actively avoid this area at night because it's dark, with lots of bushes and equipment to hide behind. It's also dangerous to walk through because of the wooden borders which are hard to see and avoid while walking at night.

This area could use:

- at least two lights to see the wood borders and any crevices
- neon paint around the wood borders (at least at each of the corners)
- trees trimmed regularly
- garden bush lights
- increased security in the area to discourage drug and alcohol activity

8. Pathway

This pathway is located at the back of the town houses (on Blake) and next to the parkette. There are lights on the top of the town houses which are too high and blocked with trees. It is a place to avoid, because of the darkness and if you screamed, people may not do anything.

"I feel a lot of people will shut the door if you are screaming or in trouble. There may be some people who would help but a lot would shut the door because they don't want to get involved. If they get involved then it's a case of 'what happens to them,' you know, do the offenders come back and torment them? You know what I'm saying? It's a tricky situation." "OK you've got neighbors but I find most people would shut the door in your face."

This area could use more and brighter lights We also need a stronger community, which we are working on with this safety audit. A safer community also makes for a stronger community.

This area, although dark and unsafe, also has some good qualities:

- lighting on top of the buildings
- fences are see-through
- people are close by (you'd have a chance if you screamed)

BLAKE STREET

This street, for our safety purposes, passed with flying colors! All the women agreed that the street was well lit, well kept, and trees and bushes were well trimmed. Frequent traffic made this street feel more safe to the women.

However, we did find some streetlights were not kept up as they should be (first and second streetlights were burned out). There also are chains across three entranceways (two on Blake Street and one on Boultbee Avenue, by apartment building) which are not brightly painted and hard to see at night.

Our suggestions would include:

- another light on the corner of the town houses at the entranceway behind 80 Blake

• neon paint or a neon plastic coating over the chains and poles

This street has undergone some changes in 1992, but through all these changes it has still stayed a seemingly safe street. The City of Toronto has put in a crosswalk, expanded the sidewalk, and planted some maple trees, which cut down on cars parking on the sidewalk/grass. The town houses all have porch lights and some have overhead spotlights at the top of the houses which makes a bright and safe atmosphere.

9. Blake Street Plaza

This plaza consists of six storefronts and it has a little laneway on each side. These laneways are dark *all* the time and are used as a hangout. There is no light in the parking lot and the mall itself has only one overhead light that is not always on. "I wouldn't come here by myself, not at night." MTHA security does not patrol this area although it is considered part of our community and has an impact on our community (e.g., drug dealers like the dark plaza in the summer).

This plaza needs more lighting in the mall itself, in the parking lot, and on each side where the laneways are.

EASTVIEW NEIGHBORHOOD COMMUNITY CENTRE

10. Parking lot

This parking lot is *very* dark. The first light was burned out, the first set of lights for the parking lot was also burned out, and the lights on the building were dim. There are signs on the wall, but they are small and hard to read. On the other end of the parking lot is a stairwell going up to Bain Avenue. These stairs are *very* dark with no lighting, it is surrounded by trees, and has no sign pointing out the staircase. "These stairs freak me out." All the women in the group avoid these stairs at night. There is a secluded slope/hill that is covered with trees/shrubs/grass. This area is *very* dark and is an extremely bad entrapment site. MTHA also does not patrol in this area.

We are suggesting:

• more and brighter lights in parking lot, staircase, and the sloping areas
• bigger/brighter signs
• trimming of trees
• neon paint strips on stairs

We found that the playground at the Blake Street Daycare Centre is very well lit. There is nowhere for anyone to hide, the fences are low and see-through. There is also some lighting at the slope in this area.

80 BLAKE STREET

11. Underground garage

In this garage we had similar observations as in the 10 Boultbee garage. As we exited the elevators to tour the garage we went through one door only to find another which we felt entrapped between. Upon walking into the garage there was an exhaust fan going which was loud, and if you were in trouble at any given time it isn't very likely that you would be heard. This area, like 10 Boultbee's garage, is also very isolated. At the time that we were down there, there were also four big garbage bins with mattresses and furniture which create a fire hazard. At this time, there were also no signs indicating which way to the stairwells or the elevators. However, there was one "Exit" sign which was blocked off by a pipe coming from the ceiling of the underground. Upon going into this garage, we noticed that the poles/corners can be hidden behind quite easily.

We asked a woman coming down with us: "How safe do you feel using this underground garage?" Her reaction was, "Oh, I don't feel safe at all. I felt happy because you're a group of women. I never use it. This is the first time by myself." Then we asked, "And why don't you use it at night by yourself?" "Why? Because I'm scared, you know, somebody . . . ," she says. "Because of drug activity or are you afraid of being attacked?" "Yeah, both."

We are suggesting the following:

- mirrors be put into the underground
- camera(s) be installed
- more signs pointing out exits and elevators
- emergency phone

12. Stairwell from garage to inside of building

As we went through the exit door on the east side of the garage we found that it also locks behind you (like at 10 Boultbee), two steps afterward is another door and yet another, about two steps apart which also locks. This makes for a *dangerous* entrapment site. Finally, after three doors, you find a caged sectioned-off area that goes down to an abandoned underground garage and stairs going up. There are no signs in this area. As we go up two flights of stairs, there is another door marked "1," with a "No Smoking" sign on the wall. There were no signs indicating where we were going along the way. You are faced with a decision of which way to go, left or right? If you weren't familiar with where the lobby was, you wouldn't know which way to go (one way is a dead end).

In this area we are suggesting:

- exit signs be put on doors coming from the garage
- signs to lobby on door and wall once through garage doors

- the rationale behind having the doors lock behind one in this area be reexamined or be told to tenants

We felt this area was very well lit and well kept. The caged sectioned-off area was also good because it prevents one from getting down to an abandoned garage.

13. Stairwell on outside of garage and second abandoned garage

This stairwell goes down to the garage ramps one and two (which is an abandoned garage). These stairs were littered with garbage and smelling of urine. On the wall of the building at the exit/entrance of the stairwell there was graffiti: a Nazi symbol with the words "You die slut". This area, in the summer, is used as a hangout for men. As we went down on the second, however, we found a circular section of the spiral ramp, which is an entrapment site. The top of this ramp (at the first garage level) is blocked off with cement blocks. So why is this stairwell not blocked off also? This entire ramp, also, has the lights smashed, so that it is quite dark at night, and in the summer, is a hangout for drug dealers and/or riffraff.

We are suggesting for this ramp the following:

- lights to be reinstalled on entire ramp
- stairwell to abandoned garage blocked off or renovated for use

14. Pathway between the town houses

As we came out of 80 Blake and started down the pathway going back to Boultbee and turned the first corner we found that it was impossible to see if anyone was there. It was also very dark with only one overhead light on a town house that was blocked by a tree. The town houses right behind have *no* lights on the exterior in their backyards which make it very dark. The parkette behind these town houses has a rope hanging down which is very dangerous. The bridge in the playground is too high for smaller children to play on. There was also quite a lot of glass in this playground and there are a lot of drinkers in this park, especially in the summer. At the bottom of the stairs leading up to Bain Avenue are garbage bins. These garbage bins are used by *all* the town houses and raccoons have been sighted in this area many times. These garbage bins are open-topped and a child could quite easily fall into them. Moving to the back of 10 Boultbee, there is no outside light above the back door. This area is dark and is also a hangout in the summertime. There is also no "entranceway" sign on the back and side doors.

For this area we are suggesting:

- corner to be better lit at back of town houses
- rope to be taken off immediately
- playground needs to be reexamined to be safer for children

- replace garbage bins with something that is safer, bigger, more attractive, and have closed top lids
- entranceway signs of doors on 10 Boultbee

Since this report many changes have been made to the parking garages at both 80 Blake and 10 Boultbee. This is good for everyone concerned, but there are several more things to be done in this neighborhood in order to make it safer to live and work in for all concerned.

Appendix 3

Safety and Security Case File

In order to improve our knowledge base, we are asking you to contribute examples of personal safety problems and solutions that you have worked on. These files will be used to revise this book, as well as to plan research and workshops on common problems. Please take the time to fill out these forms (keep a copy for your files), then return them to Gerda Wekerle, Faculty of Environmental Studies, York University, 4700 Keele Street, North York, Ontario, Canada, M3J 1P3.

Location of Site:

Identified problem(s):

How did you deal with problem(s):

Suggested solution(s):

Improvements made (when):

Was there any formal evaluation of these improvements? Should there be? Suggested means of evaluation?

Other comments:

Documentation—Please attach sketches or photographs

Contributor:

Affiliation:

Address:

Date:

Appendix 4

Evaluation of Safe Cities: Guidelines for Planning, Design, and Management

Your experience in using this book will help us in revising and improving it. After you have gone through the guide, please take a few minutes to give us your feedback. Then return this page to Gerda Wekerle, Faculty of Environmental Studies, York University, 4700 Keele Street, North York, Ontario, Canada, M3J 1P3.

1. On the whole, how useful did you find this working guide?

   _____ very useful _____ quite useful _____ not very useful

2. What sections did you refer to most often?

3. What sections did you refer to least often?

   _____

4. What additions, changes, or deletions would you make to a second edition (add additional pages as necessary)?

   _____

5. Other comments:

RESOURCES ON PLANNING AND DESIGNING SAFER ENVIRONMENTS

Background—Crime, Fear of Crime

Braungart, M. M., R. G. Braungart, and W. J. Hoyer. 1980. "Age, sex, and social factors in fear of crime." *Sociological Focus* 13(1):55–66.

Bursik, R. J. and H. G. Grasmick. 1993. *Neighborhoods and Crime: The Dimensions of Effective Community Control.* New York: Lexington Books.

The Canadian Panel on Violence Against Women. 1993. *Changing the Landscape: Ending Violence— Achieving Equality.* Ottawa: Minister of Supply and Services.

———. 1993. *The Community Kit.* Ottawa: Minister of Supply and Services.

Charland, J. 1988. *Women's Personal Security, Fear of Crime, and the Urban Environment.* Master's Major Paper, Faculty of Environmental Studies, York University, Toronto, Canada.

Charland, M. 1990. *Les Femmes et la Sécurité dans l'Environnement Urbain.* Montreal: Information resources femmes et logement.

Davis, M. 1992. "Fortress L.A." In *City of Quartz: Excavating the Future in Los Angeles.* New York: Vintage.

Felson, M. 1994. *Crime and Everyday Life: Insight and Implications for Society.* Thousand Oaks, CA.: Pine Forge Press.

Gardner, C. B. 1990. "Safe conduct: women, crime, and self in public places." *Social Problems* 37. 311–28.

Gordon, M. et al. 1980. "Crime, women, and the quality of urban life." *Signs: Journal of Women in Culture and Society* 5 (3) suppl.:S144–60.

Gordon, M., and S. Riger. 1989. *The Female Fear.* New York: The Free Press.

Grant, A. 1988. *Women and Public Urban Space: Women's Freedom of Movement in the City of Toronto.* Master's Thesis, Department of Geography, University of Toronto.

Hanmer, J., and S. Saunders. 1984. *Well-founded Fear: A Community Study of Violence to Women.* London: Hutchinson.

Home Office Standing Conference on Crime Prevention. 1989. *Report of the Working Group on the Fear of Crime.* London: Home Office.

Horton, M. J., and L. W. Kennedy. 1987. "Coping with the fear of crime." In K. Storrie (ed.), *Women: Isolation and Bonding.* Toronto: Methuen, 39–46.

LaGrange, R. L., and K. F. Ferraro. 1989. "Assessing age and gender differences in perceived risk and fear of crime." *Criminology* 27:697–718.

Macleod, L. 1989. *The City for Women: No Safe Place.* Ottawa: Corporate Policy Branch, Secretary of State Canada.

———. 1991. *Freedom from Fear: A Woman's Right, A Community Concern, A National Priority.* Ottawa: Secretary of State Canada.

Maxfield, M. G. 1984. *Fear of Crime in England and Wales.* London: HMSO.

———. 1987. *Explaining Fear of Crime.* London: HMSO.

METRAC (Metro Action Committee on Public Violence Against Women and Children) Women Plan Toronto, York University Faculty of Environmental Studies. 1987. *The Women in Safe Environments (WISE) Report.* Toronto: METRAC.

Metro Toronto Task Force on Public Violence Against Women and Children. 1984. *Final Report of the Subcommittee on Urban Design.* Toronto: Metropolitan Toronto.

Nasar, J. L., and B. Fisher. 1993. "'Hotspots' of fear and crime: a multi-method investigation." *Journal of Environmental Psychology* 13: 187–206.

Research and Forecasts, Inc. 1983. *America Afraid: How Fear of Crime Changes the Way We Live.* New York: New American Library.

Skogan, W. G. 1986. "The fear of crime and its behavioral implications." In E. A. Fattah (ed.), *From Crime Policy to Victim Policy: Reorienting the Justice System.* London: Macmillan, 167–88.

Smith, M. 1988. "Women's fear of violent crime: an exploratory test of a feminist hypothesis." *Journal of Family Violence* 3(1):29–38.

Smith, S. 1987. "Fear of crime: beyond a geography of deviance." *Progress in Human Geography* 11(1):1–23.

Solicitor General of Canada. 1985. *Canadian Urban Victimization Survey.* Bulletin No. 4: "Female Victims of Crime." Ottawa: Solicitor General Canada.

Stanko, E. A. 1988. "Fear of crime and the myth of the safe home: a feminist critique of criminology." In K. Yllo and B. M. Bogard (eds.), *Feminist Perspectives on Wife Abuse.* Newberry Park: Sage.

———. 1990. *Everyday Violence: How Women and Men Experience Sexual and Physical Danger.* London: Pandora.

Stimpson, L., and M. C. Best. 1991. *Sexual Assault Against Women With Disabilities.* Toronto: DisAbled Women's Network.

Stoks, F. 1982. *Assessing Urban Public Space Environments for Danger of Violent Crime—Especially Rape.* Ph.D. dissertation, Department of Planning, University of Washington.

Taylor, R. B. 1989. "Towards an environmental psychology of disorder: delinquency, crime, and fear of crime." In D. Stokols and I. Altman (eds.), *Handbook of Environmental Psychology* 2:951–86. New York: John Wiley.

Trevethan, S., and T. Samagh. 1992. "Gender differences among violent crime victims," *Juristat* 12(21). Ottawa: Canadian Center for Justice Statistics.

Tuan, Y. F. 1979. *Landscapes of Fear.* New York: Pantheon Books.

U.S. Department of Justice. 1990. Federal Bureau of Investigation. *Uniform Crime Reports 1990.* Washington, D.C.: U.S. Department of Justice.

Valentine, G. 1989. "The geography of women's fear," *Area* 21(4):385–90.

Warr, M. 1984. "Fear of victimization: why are women and the elderly more afraid?" *Social Science Quarterly* (65):681–702.

———. 1985. "Fear of rape among urban women," *Social Problems* 32(3):238–50.

———. 1990. "Dangerous situations: social context and fear of victimization." *Social Forces* 68:89–90.

Whitzman, C. 1988. *Women, Fear and Urban Neighborhoods.* Master's Thesis, Department of Geography, University of Toronto, Canada.

Women Plan Toronto. 1985. *Shared Experiences and Dreams: Implications for City Planning.* Toronto: Women Plan Toronto.

———. 1990. "Going to market." *Security Management* 34(10):84–87.

Planning Process

Bulos, M. 1988. "Issues of Research, Policy and Implementation." In summary of papers from conference *Women & Their Built Environment.* London, U.K.

Farish, M. 1988. "How do you ask women what they want?" In summary of papers from conference *Women & Their Built Environment*. London, U.K.

Heinzelmann, F. 1993. *The National Institute of Justice Role in Operation Weed and Seed*. Washington, D.C.: Crime Prevention and Enforcement Division, National Institute of Justice.

Holder, R., and J. Stafford. 1991. *Preventing Crime Against Women: Key Issues Arising from a National Conference*. London, U.K.: London Borough of Hammersmith and Fulham and Crime Concern.

Home Office. 1990. *Partnership in Crime Prevention*. London: HMO.

London Planning Advisory Service. 1987. *Planning for Women: An Evaluation of Consultation in Three London Boroughs*. London: London Planning Advisory Service.

Rosenbaum, D. 1986a. "The theory and research behind neighborhood watch: is it a sound fear and crime reduction strategy?" *Crime and Delinquency* 33:103–34.

———. 1986b. *Community Crime Prevention: Does It Work?* Beverly Hills: Sage.

Sarre, R. 1991. "The evaluation of crime prevention projects: issues for local government." Workshop for Local Government: Creating Safer Communities Conference. Melbourne.

Whitzman, C. 1993. "Taking back planning: promoting women's safety in public places—the Toronto experience." *Journal of Architectural and Planning Research* 9(4).

———. 1994. "In Toronto, planning is the best defense." *Planning* 60:10–11.

Wilson, J., and G. Kelling. 1983. "Broken windows: the police and neighborhood safety." In J. Wilson (ed.), *Thinking About Crime*. New York: Basic Books, 75–89.

Women's Design Service (WDS), *Planning London*. 1992. *Broadsheet on Unitary Plans*. London: Women's Design Service.

———. 1992. *Challenging Women Broadsheet on City Challenge*. London: Women's Design Service.

Crime Prevention Through Environmental Design—General

——— 1986. "Planning out the criminals." [Special Issue] *Town and Country Planning* 55(5).

Anderson, L. 1989. "Practice security design," *Alts Memo*, November, 5–6.

Archea, J. C. 1985. "The use of architectural props in the conduct of criminal acts," *Journal of Architectural and Planning Research* 2:245–59.

Association of Professional Engineers of Ontario (APEO). 1992. Task Group on Building a Safe Environment. *Phase 1: Report*. Toronto: APEO.

Behrends, J. D. 1987. "Security conscious site design," *Progressive Architecture* 68:140–42.

Bell, W. 1991. "The planning role in creating safer communities." Abstract of paper prepared for *Local Government: Creating Safer Communities*, Australian Institute of Criminology Conference. Canberra: Australian Institute of Criminology.

Brantingham, P., and P. Brantingham. 1981. *Environmental Criminology*. Beverly Hills: Sage.

———. 1988. "Situational crime prevention in British Columbia." *Journal of Security Administration* 11:17–27.

Canada Mortgage and Housing Corporation. 1983. *Evaluation of Window Guards for Resistance to Forced Entry*. Ottawa: CMHC.

Cohen, L., and M. Felson. 1979. "Social change and crime rate trends: a routine activity approach." *American Sociological Review* 44:588–608.

Coleman, A. 1985. *Utopia on Trial: Vision and Reality in Planned Housing*. London: Hilary Shipman.

Cooper M. C., and C. Francis. 1990. *People Places: Design Guidelines for Urban Open Space*. New York: Van Nostrand Reinhold.

Council of Europe. 1989. *Local Strategies for the Reduction of Urban Insecurity in Europe*. Proceedings from Standing Conference of Local & Regional Authorities of Europe (No. 35) Council of Europe: Strasbourg.

Duffala, D. 1976. "Convenience stores, armed robbery, and physical environmental features." *American Behavioral Scientist* 20:227–46.

European and North American Conference on Urban Safety and Crime Prevention. 1989. *Briefing Books* and *Agenda for Safer Cities*. Montreal: European and North American Conference on Urban Safety and Crime Prevention.

Falanga, M. 1987. "Pre-construction evaluation techniques for reducing environmentally related crime." *Design Methods and Theories* 21(4):717–22.

Geason, S., and P. Wilson. 1989. *Designing out Crime: Crime Prevention Through Environmental Design*. Canberra: Australian Institute of Criminology.

Government of Australia. 1991. *Local Government: Creating Safer Communities, Report on National Conference*. Melbourne: Government of Australia.

Guterson, D. 1993. "Home, safe home: what lurks behind the walls in America's new high security suburbs." *Utne Reader* 56:62–67.

Heck, S. 1987. "Oscar Newman revisited." *Architects Journal* 8:30–32.

Hedberg, N. A. 1987. "Be active—not reactive—with preventative security." *Buildings* 81:72–75.

Hillier, B. 1973. "In defence of space." *RIBA Journal* 8(11):539–44.

Hillier, B., and J. Hanson. 1984. *The Social Logic of Space*. Cambridge: Cambridge University Press.

Jacobs, J. 1961. *The Death and Life of Great American Cities*. New York: Random House.

Jeffrey, C. R. 1977. *Crime Prevention Through Environmental Design*. Beverly Hills: Sage Publications.

Kennedy, D. B. 1990. "Facility site selection and analysis through environmental criminology." *Journal of Criminal Justice* 18:239–52.

Maltz, M. D., A. C. Gordon, and W. Friedman. 1990. *Mapping Crime in its Community Setting: Event Geography Analysis*. New York: Springer-Verlag.

METRAC. 1991. *Developing a Safe Urban Environment for Women: Discussion Paper*. Toronto: METRAC.

National Association of Local Government Women's Committees. 1991. *Responding with Authority*. Birmingham, U.K.: National Association of Local Government Women's Committees.

Newman, O. 1972. *Defensible Space*. New York: Macmillan.

Nydele, A. 1986. "Practice: Designing for terrorism and other aggressions." *Architectural Record* 174:37–43.

Pacquette, D. 1991. "In-service training." *WEB: Women and the Built Environment*, Spring/Summer.

Painter, K. 1988. *Lighting and Crime Prevention: The Edmonton Project*. U.K.: Middlesex Polytechnic.

Poyner, B. 1984. *Design Against Crime: Beyond Defensible Space*. London: Butterworths.

Rand, G. 1984. "Crime and environment: a review of the literature and its implications for urban architecture and planning." *Journal of Architectural Planning and Research* 1:3–19.

Rosenbaum, D., ed. 1986. *Community Crime Prevention: Does It Work?* Beverly Hills: Sage.

Rubenstein, H., C. Murray, T. Motoyama, and W. V. Rouse. 1980. *The Link Between Crime and the Built Environment*. Washington, D.C.: The Law Enforcement Assistance Administration, National Institute of Justice.

Schlomo, A. 1968. *Discouraging Crime Through City Planning*. Working Paper No. 17. Berkeley: University of California, Berkeley, Institute of Urban and Regional Planning.

Sherman, L. W., P. R. Gartin, and M. E. Buerger. 1989. "Hot spots of predatory crime: routine activities and the criminology of place." *Criminology* 27:27–55.

Siemonsen, K., and G. Zauke. 1991. *Sicherheit im Oeffentlichen Raum: Städtebauliche und planerische Massnahmen zur Verminderung von Gewalt* (*Safety in Open Space: Design and Planning Measures to Mitigate Force*). Zurich: edition ebersbach in efef-Verlag AG. (Available from FOPA, Dortmund, Germany.)

Sinnott, R. 1985. *Safety and Security in Building Design*. New York: Van Nostrand Reinhold.

Spicker, P. 1987. "Poverty and depressed estates: a critique of Utopia on Trial." *Housing Studies* 2(4):283–92.

Stoks, F. 1986. "Assessing urban public space environments for danger of violent crime, especially rape." In D. Joiner, et al. (eds.), *Conference on People and Physical Environment Research*. Wellington, N. Z.: Ministry of Works and Development, 331–42.

Taskforce on Security Design. 1989. *Bibliography on Building Security*. (Nos. 153, 174) Washington, D.C.: American Institute of Architects.

Taylor, R. A., and J. R. Hancock. 1990. "Don't segregate—integrate." *Security Management* 34:23–24.

Taylor, R. B., S. Gottfredson, and S. Brower. 1980. "The defensibility of defensible space: a critical review and synthetic framework for future research." In M. Gottfredson and T. Hirschi (eds.), *Understanding Crime: Current Theory and Research*. New York: Sage.

Trench, S., T. Oc, and S. Tiesdell. 1991. "Safer cities for women—perceived risks and planning measures." Institute of Planning Studies, University of Nottingham, U.K.

Underwood, G. 1984. *The Security of Buildings*. London: Architectural Press.

Valentine, G. 1990. "Women's fear and the design of public space." *Built Environment* 16(4):288–303.

Von Nyl, A., et al. 1993. *Frau, Stadt, Angst, Raum* (*Women, City, Fear, Space*). Zurich: Frauenlobby Städtebau.

Waller, I. 1989. *Current Trends in European Crime Prevention: Implications for Canada*. Ottawa: Department of Justice.

Women's Design Service. 1990. *At Her Convenience*. London: Women's Design Service.

——— "Tenant revolt over Coleman Master Plan" 1986. *Architects Journal* 12:34.

Cities and Crime Prevention Through Environmental Design

Amsterdam Physical Planning Department. 1985. *Physical Planning and the Emancipation of Women*. Amsterdam: Physical Planning Department.

Brisbane City Council. n.d. *Safety Audits: Making Your Community Safer*. Brisbane, Australia: City Council.

Council of Europe. 1989. Standing Conference of Local and Regional Authorities of Europe. *Local Strategies for the Reduction of Urban Insecurity in Europe*, Strasbourg: Council of Europe.

Dubrow, G. L., et al. 1986. "Planning to end violence against women: notes from a feminist conference at UCLA." *Women and Environments* 8(2):4–9.

City of Toronto. 1989. *Section of the Housing By-law Regarding Storage Garages in Multiple Occupancy Dwellings*. Toronto: City of Toronto Buildings and Inspection Department.

City of Toronto Planning and Development Department. 1990. *Design Guidelines for Underground Tunnels*. Toronto: City of Toronto Planning and Development Department.

———. 1990. *Planning for a Safer City*. CityPlan Background Report No. 10. Toronto: City of Toronto Planning and Development Department.

———. 1991. *CityPlan Proposals Report*. Toronto: City of Toronto Planning and Development Department.

City of Toronto Planning and Development Department, and Gerda R. Wekerle. 1992. *A Working Guide for Planning and Designing Safer Urban Environments*. Toronto: Safe City Committee and City of Toronto Planning and Development Department.

City of Toronto Safe City Committee. 1988. *The Safe City: Municipal Strategies for Preventing Public Violence Against Women*. Toronto: Safe City Committee.

———. 1991. *A Safer City: The Second Stage Report of the Safe City Committee*. Toronto: Safe City Committee.

Commissioner of Planning and Development. 1993. "A Working Guide for Planning and Designing Safer Urban Environments and the Site Plan Approval Process." Toronto: City of Toronto Planning and Development Department.

Greater London Council Women's Committee. 1986. *Changing Places: Positive Action on Women and Planning*. London: GLC.

Halton Regional Police. 1986. *Crime Prevention Through Environmental Design Manual*. Brampton: Halton Regional Police.

Home Office Crime Prevention Unit. 1990. *Safer Cities Progress Report 1989–1990*. London, U.K.: Home Office.

———. 1991. *Safer Cities Progress Report 1990–1991*. London, U.K.: Home Office.

———. 1991. *Safer Communities: The Local Delivery of Crime Prevention Through the Partnership Approach*. Prepared for Standing Conference on Crime Prevention. London, U.K.: Home Office.

Islington Safer Cities Project. 1990. *Women and Safety in Islington*. Islington Council, U.K.

Jones, T., B. MacLean, and J. Young. 1986. *The Islington Crime Survey*. London: Gower Press.

Kendrick, T. 1991. "Creating safer neighbourhoods: the British experience." Presentation for Local Government: Creating Safer Communities Conference, Melbourne.

Leicester City Council and Leicestershire Constabulary. 1989. Crime Prevention by Planning and Design. Leicester, U.K.: City Council.

London Borough of Haringey. 1987. *A Guide for Developers: Towards a Safer Environment*. Haringey U.K.: City Council.

London Borough of Wandsworth. 1986. *Planning Design Guidelines: Personal Safety and Security*. Wandsworth, U.K.: City Council.

Manchester City Planning Department. 1987. *Planning a Safer Environment for Women*. Manchester, U.K.: City Planning Department.

Manchester City Council. 1987. *Manchester's Crime Survey of Women for Women—Women and Violence Survey Report*. Manchester: Manchester City Council Police Monitoring Unit.

Merry, S. 1981. "Defensible space undefended: social factors in crime control through environmental design." *Urban Affairs Quarterly* 16(4):397–422.

Ministry of Housing, Physical Planning and the Environment. 1986. *Urban Planning and Community Safety*. The Hague, Netherlands: Ministry of Housing, Physical Planning and the Environment.

National Committee on Violence. 1990. *Violence: Directions for Australia*. Canberra: Australian Institute of Criminology.

National Crime Prevention Council. 1994. *Consultation Document*. Ottawa: Community Safety and Crime Prevention Unit, Department of Justice.

National Safe Neighbourhoods [NACRO]. 1989. *Crime Prevention and Community Safety: A Practical Guide for Local Authorities*. London: NACRO.

Nottingham Safer Cities Project. 1990. *Community Safety in Nottingham City Centre*. Report of the Steering Group. Nottingham, U.K.: Nottingham Council.

Rand, G. 1983. *Crime and Environment: An Approach for Los Angeles*. Urban Innovations Group, University of California in Los Angeles.

Southampton City Council. *Safety of Women in Public Places: Results of the Survey*. Southampton, U.K.: Directorate of Planning and Development.

Tandem Montreal. 1991. *Par le Trou de la Serrure* (review in French of some European and North American safe city initiatives) 2(1). Montreal, November.

Wandsworth Safer Cities Project. 1991. *Progress Report and Action Plan 1991/92*. Wandsworth, U.K.: Wandsworth Council.

Weeber, L. 1993. *Preliminary Report on Safety Audits of the Pakuranga Ward*. Manukan Safer Community Council, N.Z., February.

West End Forum Project. 1991. *Final Report*. Melbourne, Australia: City of Melbourne.

Whitzman, C. 1989. "Letter from the Netherlands." *Women and Environments* 11(3/4):14–15.

Winnipeg Police Department. n.d. *Crime Prevention Environmental Design Guidelines: A Qualitative Checklist*. Winnipeg: Winnipeg Police Department.

Winnipeg Social Planning Council. 1991. *A Safer Winnipeg for Women and Children*. Winnipeg: Social Planning Council.

Safer Transportation

Atkins, S. T. 1989. *Critical Paths: Designing for Secure Travel*. London: Design Council.

———. 1990. "Personal security as a transport issue: a state of the art review." *Transport Reviews* 10(2):111–25.

Beller, A., S. Garellk, and S. Cooper. 1980. "Sex crimes in the subway." *Criminology* 18(1):35–52.

Brewer, M., and C. Davis. 1988. "Making transport facilities meet women's needs." In summary of papers from conference *Women & their Built Environment*. London, U.K.

Brög, W. 1987. *Delinquency and Vandalism in Public Transport*, European Conference of Ministers of Transport, Economic Research Center, Round Table 77.

City of Saint Paul, Minnesota. 1991. An ordinance amending Chapter 417 of the Saint Paul Legislative Code relating to safety requirements for licensed parking lots.

EnTRA Consultants. 1991. "Security of Women on GO Transit: Proposal," Toronto, July.

Evans, M. 1982. "Ending the curfew on women," *London Labor Briefing* 21:24–25, July. Reprinted in *Women and Environments* 6(2):14, April 1984.

Frankl, V. 1983. "London's model for making a city safe." *Ms* 11(8):21, February.

George Rand Associates. 1984. *Crime Analysis of SCRTD Metro Rail Project: Technical Report*. George Rand Associates: Los Angeles, CA.

Greater London Council Women's Committee. 1984–1987. *Women on the Move: GLC Survey on Women and Transport* (9 volumes). London: GLC.

Groeger, J. A. 1991. *Relative Risks of Taxi and Minicab Use—A Summary of the Technical Report*. London: The Suzy Lamplugh Trust, July.

———. 1991. *Expectations and Experience of Taxi and Minicab Use—Technical Report*. London: The Suzy Lamplugh Trust, July.

King, M. 1988. *How to Make Social Crime Prevention Work: The French Experience*. London: National Association for the Care and Resettlement of Offenders.

Levine, N., and M. Wachs. 1985. *Factors Affecting the Incidence of Bus Crime in Los Angeles*. Washington, D.C.: U.S. Department of Transportation, Urban Mass Transportation Administration.

Local Transport Today. 1990. "Easing women's travel fears: a suitable case for special treatment?" October 17.

London Borough of Hackney. 1991. "Hackney mini-cab scheme." Hackney, U.K., February.

Lynch, G., and S. Atkins. 1987. "The influence of personal security fears on women's travel patterns." UTSG Conference, Sheffield University, January.

Mancini, A. N., and R. Jain. 1987. "Commuting parking lots—vandalism and deterrence." *Transportation Quarterly* 41(4):539–53.

Market Facts of Canada Limited. 1991. *Summary of Findings: Designated Waiting Areas Program Preliminary Site Testing*. Toronto: Toronto Transit Commission.

Metropolitan Transportation Authority. 1988. *Crime and Personal Security in the Subway: New Yorkers' Perceptions*. N.Y.: MTA.

———. 1990. *TA Tracking Surveys—April 1989–February 1990*. N.Y.: MTA.

———. 1989. *New Yorkers' Perceptions of Subway and Bus Service: A Tracking Study*. N.Y.: MTA.

Ohlenschlager, S. 1990. "Women also travel." In S. Trench and T. Oc (eds.), *Current Issues in Planning*. Brookfield, VT: Gower, 26–32.

Oxley, P. R. 1987. "Assaults on bus staff in Great Britain." *Transportation Research Record* 1108:27.

Pearlstein, A., and M. Wachs. 1982. "Crime in public transit systems: an environmental design perspective." *Transportation* 11(4):277–90.

Project for Public Spaces, Inc. 1984. *Times Square Subway Station: Security and Public Use*. N.Y.: Project for Public Spaces.

Rutherford, B. M., and G. R. Wekerle. 1987. "Captive rider, captive labor: spatial constraints and women's employment." *Urban Geography* 9(2):116–37.

Saville, Gregory J. 1991. "Transdisciplinarity, environmental criminology and the Toronto Subway Security Audit." *Security Journal* 2(4):219–26.

Spring, G. (Melbourne Public Transport Commission). 1991. "Public transport safety: a community right and communal responsibility." Paper presented at conference *Local Government: Creating Safer Communities*. Melbourne, Australia, November.

Toronto Transit Commission, METRAC, Metro Toronto Police Force. 1989. *Moving Forward: Making Transit Safer for Women*. Toronto: TTC.

TTC, METRAC, MTPF, City of Scarborough, Scarborough Women's Action Network. 1991. *Making Transit Stops Safer for Women: Scarborough Moves Forward*. Toronto: TTC.

Van Wijk, J. 1986. *From Structure Plan to Realization of Station Sloerdijk: Social Safety in Practice*. Amsterdam, Netherlands: Physical Planning Department.

Safer Housing—Design

Anson, B. 1986. "Removing walkways is not nearly enough." *Town & Country Planning* 55:174–75.

———. 1987. "Battling for the right to design their homes." *Town & Country Planning* 56(3):69–70.

Avery, H. 1989. "Safe housing for women: Mavis/McMullen Place." *WEB: Women and the Built Environment*.

———. 1989. "Sitka Housing Co-operative: women house themselves." *Women and Environments* 11(2):19–21.

Black and Moffat Architects. 1990. *Toward Drug Resistant Urban Housing: Report of a Literature Search*. Report prepared for Moss Park Community Development Project. Toronto: Moss Park Community Development Project.

Canada Mortgage and Housing Corporation. 1989. *Overview of CMHC Activities Related to Urban Safety and Crime Prevention*. Ottawa: CMHC.

———. 1989b. *A Synthesis of International Literature on Urban Safety and Crime Prevention in Residential Environments: Interim Report and Bibliography*. Ottawa: CMHC.

Coleman, A. 1986. "Design improvement: utopia goes on trial." *Town and Country Planning* 55(5):138.

Cooper M. C., and W. Sarkissian. 1986. *Housing as if People Mattered: Site Design Guidelines for Medium-Density Housing*. Berkeley: University of California Press.

Dillon, D. 1994. "Fortress America." *Planning* 60: 8–12.

Linden, R., and Prairie Research Associates Inc. 1990. *Crime Prevention and Urban Safety in Residential Environments: Final Report*. Ottawa: CMHC.

London Borough of Haringey. 1987. *Safety by Design: Borough Initiatives in Housing Design with Particular Reference to the Safety and Security of Women.* Haringey, U.K.: Council.

London Borough of Southwark. 1985. *Housing Security Design Guide.* Southwark, U.K.: Council.

Meredith, C. 1988. *Apartment Crime Prevention Project: Report of Research Findings.* Ottawa: Solicitor General Canada, No. 1988–09, User Report.

Moughtin, J. C., and A. Gardner. 1990. "Towards an improved and protected environment." *The Planner* 76(22):9–12.

———. 1989. *Safer Neighborhoods: Re-designing Housing Developments to Reduce Crime and Enhance Community Safety.* York, U.K.: University of York, Institute of Advanced Architectural Studies.

Popkin, S. et al. 1993. *An Evaluation of the Chicago Housing Authority's Public Housing Drug Elimination Program.* Chicago: Loyola University, Department of Criminal Justice.

Task Force on Security Design. 1989. *Bibliography on Building Security* (Nos. 153, 174). Washington, D.C.: American Institute of Architects.

Vogel-Heffernan, M. 1986. "Designing battered women's shelters." *Women and Environments Magazine* 8(2):7.

Ware, V. 1987. "Problem with design improvements at home." *Town and Country Planning* 56(10):264–66.

———. 1988. *Women's Safety on Housing Estates.* London: Women's Design Service.

Warren, F., and P. Stollard. 1988. *Safe as Houses.* York, U.K.: The Institute of Advanced Architectural Studies.

Whitzman, C. 1989. "Community and design: against the solution in St. James Town." *City Magazine* 11(1):32–36.

Safer Housing—Community Crime Prevention

Andrew, C., F. Klodowsky, and C. Lundy. 1992. "Housing and community planning research and the issue of violence against women." Paper presented at International Housing Conference, Montreal. (Available from Department of Political Science, University of Ottawa.)

Appleyard, D. 1981. *Livable Streets.* Berkeley: University of California Press

Brown, K. 1979. "Connecting vision–grid planning." *Architectural Review* 165:227–39.

Bulos, M., and S. Walker. 1988. "A call for intensive management: the U.K. experience." In N. Teymur, T. A. Marcus and T. Woolley (eds.), *Rehumanizing Housing.* London: Butterworths, pp. 101–11.

Eagan, A. B. 1987. "The Girl in 1–A: sexual harassment hits home." *Mademoiselle*, April.

Eubank-Ahrens, B. 1987. "A closer look at users of woonerven." In A. Vernon Moudon (ed.), *Public Streets for Public Use.* New York: Columbia University Press, 63–79.

Fowler, E. P. 1987. "Street management and city design." *Social Forces* 66(2):365–89.

Francis, M. 1987. "The making of democratic streets." In A. Vernez Moudon (ed.), *Public Streets for Public Use.* New York: Columbia University Press, 23–39.

Greenberg, S. W., A. R. Williams, and W. M. Rohe. 1982. "Safety in urban neighborhoods: a comparison of physical characteristics and informal territorial control in high and low crime neighborhoods." *Population and Environment* 5:141–65.

Greenberg, S. W. 1986. "Fear and its relationship to crime, neighborhood deterioration, and informal social control." In J. M. Bryne and R. J. Simpson (eds.), *The Social Ecology of Crime.* New York: Springer-Verlag, 47–62.

Hunter, A., and T. L. Baumer. 1982. "Street traffic, social integration, and fear of crime." *Sociological Inquiry* 52(2):122–31.

Jim Ward Associates. 1991. *Moss Park Community Development Project: Community Consultation Report*, Toronto: Moss Park Community Development Project.

Kail, B. L., and P. H. Kleinman. 1985. "Fear, crime, community organization, and limitation on daily routines." *Urban Affairs Quarterly* 20(3):400–408.

London Housing Unit. n.d. *Guidelines for Dealing with Racial and Sexual Harassment in Temporary Accomodation.* London.

Mahaddie, A. 1976. "Why the grid roads wiggle." *Architectural Design* 46(9):539–42.

Mayor's Task Force on Drugs. 1989. *Report of the Neighbourhood Action on Drugs Forum.* Toronto: City of Toronto.

Metro Toronto Housing Authority. 1991. *Homewords.* Toronto: MTHA.

Moudon, A. V. 1987. *Public Streets for Public Use.* New York: Columbia University Press.

National Action Committee on the Status of Women Housing Committee. 1991. *Women and Housing: Creating Solidarity.* Toronto: NAC.

Novac, S. and Associates. 1993. *The Security of Her Person: Tenants' Experiences of Sexual Harassment.* Toronto: Ontario Women's Directorate and Ministry of Housing.

Ontario Non-Profit Housing Association. 1991. *Access for Women Who Are Experiencing Violence* (Report 91–02). Toronto: Ontario Non-Profit Housing Association.

Pader, E. J., and M. M. Breitbart. 1993. "Transforming public housing: conflicting visions for Harbor Point." *Places* 8:34–41.

Pettersson, G. 1988. "Safety on estates and other problem areas." In summary of papers from conference *Women & their Built Environment.* London, U.K.

Rahder, Doyle and Associates, and Jim Ward Associates. 1992. *City Home Security Policy/Strategy Study.* Toronto: City of Toronto Housing Department.

Rao, N. 1990. "Public housing: inequal opportunities." *WEB: Women and the Built Environment,* Winter.

Roncek, D., and A. Lobosco. 1983. "The effect of high schools on crime in their neighborhoods." *Social Science Quarterly* 64:598–613.

Rosenbaum, D. 1988. "Community crime prevention: a review and synthesis of the literature." *Justice Quarterly* 15:323–94.

Sanford, B. 1988. *St. James Town Revitalization: Social Analysis.* Toronto: City of Toronto Planning and Development Department.

Shearing, C. 1989. *MTHA Security Delivery System: A Blueprint for Change: The Lessons of the Pilot Projects.* Toronto: MTHA.

Solicitor General Canada. 1983. *The Good Neighbors Crime Prevention Handbook.* Ottawa: Solicitor General Canada.

Stahwra, J. 1986. "Suburban crime." *Security Systems Administration* 15:26–27, 40–41.

Stollard, P., S. Osborn, H. Shaftoe, and K. Croucher. 1989. *Safer Neighborhoods.* York, U.K.: The Institute of Advanced Architectural Studies.

Taylor, R. B., S. A. Shumaker, and S. D. Gottredson. 1985. "Neighborhood level links between physical features and local sentiments: deterioration, fear of crime, and confidence." *Journal of Architecture and Planning Research* 2:261–75.

Teymur, N., T. A. Marcus, and T. Woolley. 1988. *Rehumanizing Housing.* Toronto: Butterworths.

Unger, D., and A. Wandersman. 1985. "The importance of neighbours: the social, cognitive, and affective components of neighboring." *American Journal of Community Psychology* 13(2):139–69.

Vergara, C. 1991. "New York's new ghettos." *The Nation,* 804–10.

Ward, J. 1991. *Report of the St. James Town Anti-Drug Community Support Pilot Project* and interim reports prepared for the Mayor's Task Force on Drugs. Toronto, September.

Weidemann, S., J. R. Anderson, and D. Butterfield. 1983. "Resident perceptions of satisfaction and safety: a basis for change in multi-family housing." *Environment and Behavior* 14(6):695–724.

Wekerle, G., and S. Novac. 1991. *Gender and Housing In Toronto*. Toronto: Women and Work Institute, Equal Opportunity Division, City of Toronto.

Safer Parks and Urban Open Space

Andropogon Associates. 1989. *Landscape Management and Restoration Program for the Woodlands of Central Park*. Report for Central Park Administration, New York City.

Belan, J. 1991. "Safety and security in High Park, Toronto: a case study." *Landscape Architectural Review* 12(3):19–21.

Burgess, J., C. M. Harrison, and M. Limb. 1988. "People, parks and the urban green: a study of popular meanings and values for open spaces in the City." *Urban Studies* 25:455–73.

Burlakow, K. 1990. *Concerns Regarding Problems of Violence and Vandalism: submission to Winnipeg Parks Department*. Winnipeg: Parks Department.

Campbell, A., M. Armstrong, and J. McKechnie. 1991. *Every Picture Tells a Story: Regeneration in Woodlands Area*. Glasgow, U.K.: Safe Castlemilk.

Chapin, D. 1991. "Making green spaces safer places: experiences in New York City," *Landscape Architectural Review* 12(3):16–18.

Citizens Taskforce on the Use and Security of Central Park. 1990. *Central Park: The Heart of the City*. New York: Central Park Conservancy.

City of Toronto: Department of Parks and Recreation. 1992. *High Park: Draft Proposals for Restoration and Management*. Toronto: City Department of Parks and Recreation.

City of Toronto Planning and Development, and Parks and Recreation Departments. 1990. *Green Spaces/Safer Places: A Forum on Planning Safer Parks for Women*. Toronto.

Cranz, G. 1980. "Women in urban parks." *Signs: Journal of Women in Culture and Society* 5(3) suppl.: 579–95.

Dandavino, R. R. 1991. "Safety and security in Mount Royal Park, Montreal." *Landscape Architectural Review* 12(3):22–24.

Egan, J. A. 1991. "Breaking through the myth of public safety: the role of user studies in park design." *Landscape Architectural Review* 12(3):7–10.

Fletcher, J. E. 1983. "Assessing the impact of actual and perceived safety and security problems on park use and enjoyment." *Journal of Park and Recreation Administration* 1(2):21–36.

Francis, M. 1987a. "Urban open spaces." In E. H. Zube and G.T. Moore (eds.), *Advances in Environment, Behavior, and Design*. New York: Plenum Press.

———. 1987b. "Some different meanings attached to a city park and community gardens." *Landscape Journal* 6(2):101–11.

———. 1989. "Control as a dimension of public space quality." In I. Altman and E. Zube (eds.), *Public Places and Spaces*. New York: Plenum.

Franck, K. A., and L. Paxson. 1989. "Women and urban public space." In I. Altman and E. H. Zube (eds.), *Public Places and Spaces*. New York: Plenum.

Harrison, C., and J. Burgess. 1989. "Living spaces." *Landscape Design*, September, 14–16.

Khong, J. 1991. "The community park users survey: a partnership approach to the planning process." *Landscape Architectural Review* 12(3):10–13.

Landscape Architectural Review 12(2). (Special issue on parks safety), July 1991.

Lueck, T. J. 1990. "Are plazas public boons, or nuisances?" *New York Times*, Section 10, October 7, I and II.

METRAC. 1989. *Planning for Sexual Assault Prevention: Women's Safety in High Park*. Toronto: METRAC.

Mozingo, L. 1989. "Women and downtown open spaces." *Places: A Quarterly Journal of Environmental Design* 6(1):38–47.

New York City Parks and Recreation Department. n.d. "Junior Ranger Naturalist Program." (pamphlet)

———. n.d. "New York Road Runner's Club Safety Program for Central Park." (pamphlet)

———. n.d. "Safety Tips for Central Park." (pamphlet)

Orsini, D. 1990. *Mitigating Fear in the Landscape: Recommendations for Enhancing Users' Perceptions of Safety in Urban Parks*. Master's Thesis, Department of Landscape Architecture, University of Guelph, Canada.

———. 1993. "Natural areas: places of beauty and fear." *Toronto Field Naturalist*, May, 13–14.

Project for Public Spaces, Inc. 1981. *Bryant Park: Intimidation or Recreation*. New York: Project for Public Spaces.

Schroeder, H. W., and L. M. Anderson. 1984. "Perception of personal safety in urban recreation sites." *Journal of Leisure Research* 16:178–94.

Storey, K. 1991. "The safety of public open space: three arguments for design." *Landscape Architectural Review* 12(3):13–16.

Thomas, S. 1991. *Allen Gardens Revitalization Study*. Design Thesis, Department of Landscape Architecture, University of Guelph, Canada.

Tuan, Y. F. 1979. *Landscapes of Fear*. New York: Pantheon.

Wekerle, G. R. 1991. "Planning safer parks for women: a new agenda for open space policy in Toronto." *Landscape Architectural Review* 12(3):5–7.

Westover, T. 1986. "Park use and perception: gender differences." *Journal of Park and Recreation Administration* 4(2).

Wineman, J., C. Zimring, J. Archea, D. H. Hayes, and J. Sanford. 1986. *Improving Park Security: Perception and Reality*. Atlanta, Ga.: Department of Parks, Recreation, and Cultural Affairs.

Safer Urban Cores

Bell, W. 1991. *Urban Design and Crime Prevention in the Adelaide CBD*. Prepared for the Crime Prevention and Criminology Unit, South Australia Attorney-General's Department for the Inner City Co-operative Action Group. Adelaide, Australia: South Australia Department of Attorney General.

Brantingham, P., P. Brantingham, and P. Wong. 1990. "Malls and crimes: a first look." *Security Journal* 1:175–81.

City of Melbourne, and the Victorian Government. 1991. "Melbourne's westend nightspots: safe enjoyment for everyone: a code of practice." (pamphlet) Melbourne.

City of Toronto. n.d. "Underground Garages: guidelines for owners and users." (pamphlet)

Hundt, R. M., and W. C. Arons. 1985. "Planning parking protection." *Security Management* 29:44–47.

Landry, C., and K. Worpole. 1991. "Revitalising public life." *Landscape Design*, April.

Minneapolis Department of Regulatory Services. 1991. "Guidelines for existing parking ramp facilities and new construction." Minneapolis: Department of Regulatory Services.

Poyner, B. 1981. "Crime prevention and the environment: street attacks in city centers." *Police Research Bulletin*, Autumn, 10–18.

Project for Public Spaces. 1984. *Managing Downtown Public Spaces*. Chicago: Planners Press, American Planning Association.

Roncek, D. 1981–1982. "Bars, blocks and crimes." *Journal of Environmental Systems* 11:35–47.

Roti, R. 1982. *Security Considerations for Parking Facilities*. Washington, D.C.: National Park Association.

Sherman, L. 1989. "Violent stranger crime at a large hotel: a case study in risk assessment methods." *Security Journal* 1:40–46.

Sijpkes, P., D. Brown, and M. LacLean. "The behavior of elderly people in Montreal's 'Indoor City'." *Plan Canada* 23(1):14–22.

Whyte, W. 1988. *City: Rediscovering the Center.* New York: Doubleday.

———. 1980. *The Social Life of Small Urban Spaces.* Washington, D.C.: The Conservation Foundation.

Women Plan Toronto. 1991. "Evaluation of Underpasses According to METRAC's Women's Safety Audit Kit." Toronto: Women Plan Toronto.

Safer Campuses

Bausell, C., and C. Maloy. 1990. *The Links Among Drugs, Alcohol and Campus Crime, A Research Report.* Towson State University: The Towson State University Center for the Study and Prevention of Campus Violence.

De Keseredy, W. 1990. *Woman Abuse in Dating Relationships: The Role of Male Peer Support.* Toronto: Canadian Scholars Press.

Fisher, B., and J. Nasar. 1992. "Fear of crime in relation to three exterior site features: prospect, refuge and escape." *Environment and Behavior* 24:35–65.

House Report 101 883, Section 201–205. 1990. *Student Right to Know and Campus Security* Act. 101 St. Congress, Second Session, Washington, D.C.

Johnston, N., and C. Polster. "Report on the safety and security of graduate women at York University." In York University Task Force on the Status of Women Graduate Students. *Not Satisfied Yet: Report of the Task Force on the Status of Women Graduate Students,* 75–91. North York, Ontario: York University.

Kelly, K., and W. S. De Keseredy. 1993 *Women's Fear of Crime and Abuse in College and University Dating Relationships.* Ottawa: Health and Welfare Canada, Family Violence Prevention Division.

Kirk, N. 1988. "Factors affecting perceptions of safety in a campus environment." In J. Sime (ed.), *Safety in the Built Environment.* London: E. and F. Spon, 285–96.

———. 1989. *Factors Affecting Perceptions of Social Safety in Public Open Space.* Thesis, Master of Landscape Architecture, University of Illinois, Champaign-Urbana.

Klodawsky, F., and C. Lundy. 1991. "Feeling safe on campus: women's safety in the university environment," Canadian Women's Studies conference, Kingston, Ontario. (Available from Klodawsky, Department of Geography, Carleton University, Ottawa, Ontario.)

Koss, M. P., C. A. Gidycz, and N. Wisniewski. 1987. "The scope of rape: incidence and prevalence of sexual aggression and victimization in a national sample of higher education students." *Journal of Counselling and Clinical Psychology* 55(2):162–70.

Leach, B., E. Lesiuk, and P. E. Morton. 1986. "Perceptions of fear in the urban environment." *Women and Environments* 8(2):10–13.

Lott, B., M. E. Reilly, and D. R. Howard. 1982. "Sexual assault and harassment: a campus community case study." *Signs* 8:296–319.

Malette, L., and M. Chalouh. 1991. *The Montreal Massacre.* Charlottetown, Prince Edward Island: Gynergy Books.

Matthews, A. 1993. "The campus crime wave: the ivory tower becomes an armed camp." *New York Times Magazine,* March 7, 38ff.

METRAC (Metro Action Committee on Public Violence Against Women and Children), and Council of Ontario Universities Committee on the Status of Women. *Women's Campus Safety Audit Guide,* Toronto: METRAC.

Morris, R. 1989. "Safety problems and sexual harassment on campus." In C. Filteau (ed.), *Women in Graduate Studies in Ontario: Proceedings of a Conference on Women in Graduate Studies in Ontario.* Toronto: Ontario Council of Graduate Studies, 13–27.

Nasar, J. L., and B. Fisher. 1991. "Hot spots of fear of crime at the micro and macro scale." Paper presented at the 23rd Environmental Design Research Association Conference, Boulder, Colorado, April. (Available from Nasar, Department of City and Regional Planning, Ohio State University.)

————. 1992. "Design for vulnerability: cues and reactions to fear of crime." *Sociology and Social Research* 76:48–58.

Paludi, M. A. 1987. *Ivory Power: Sexual Harassment on Campus.* Albany: State University of New York Press.

Raddatz, A. 1988. *Crime on Campus: Institutional Tort Liability for the Criminal Acts of Third Parties.* Washington, D.C.: National Association of College and University Attorneys.

Ramazanoglu, C. 1987. "Sex and violence in academic life, or, you can keep a good woman down." In J. Hanmer and M. Maynard (eds.), *Women, Violence and Social Control.* London: Macmillan, 61–74.

Sanday, P. R. 1990. *Fraternity Gang Rape: Sex, Brotherhood and Privilege on Campus.* New York: NYU Press.

Smith, M. C. 1988. *Coping with Crime on Campus.* New York: Macmillan.

Safer Workplaces

B.C. Federation of Labor, and the Women's Research Centre. 1992. *Taking Action: A Union Guide to Ending Violence Against Women.* Vancouver, B.C.: Federation of Labor.

City of Toronto Parks and Recreation Department. 1991. *Facility Safety Audit Summary.* Toronto: City of Toronto Parks and Recreation Department.

Edmonton Police Department. n.d. "Working alone: security in the workplace."

Hetherton, M. "The other office hazard," *WEB: Women & the Built Environment* 14:3.

Hierlihy, D. 1993. *Ensuring Equitable Client Service Throughout the City: Community Workplace Safety Program Advisory Committee, Final Report.* Toronto: Home Care Program for Metropolitan Toronto, August.

Rozelle, G. 1992. "Is homecare a dangerous occupation?." *Caring Magazine* (April):50–53.

Swanton, B. 1989. *Violence and Public Contact Workers.* National Committee on Violence, Violence Today Bulletin #5. Woden: Australian Institute of Criminology.

Security and Liability

Angel, C. 1991. "USC nurse wins $1.8 million for injuries in campus attack: firing sparks new suit." *Los Angeles Daily Journal* 104:1.

Anthony, A. J., and F. F. Thornburg. 1989. "Security on trial." *Security Management* 33(2):41–46, February.

Ballou, G. M. 1981. "Recourse for rape victims: third party liability." *Harvard Women's Law Journal* 4:105–160.

Blodgett, N. 1987. "Lusting landlords." *American Bar Association Journal* 73(2):30.

Brown, K. M. 1983. "California landlords' duty to protect tenants from criminals." *San Diego Law Review* 20:859–73.

Butler, C. 1989. "Sexual harassment in rental housing." *University of Illinois Law Review* 1(1):175–214.

Canton, Lucien, G. 1990. "Limiting liability exposure: have we gone too far?" *Security Management* 34(1):71–72.

Cherry, R. L. 1984. "Liability of business property owners for injury to customers in parking lots by criminal attacks from third parties." *Real Estate Law Journal* 13:141–58.

Cohen, R. 1987. "Home is no haven: an analysis of sexual harassment in housing," *Wisconsin Law Review* 1 (6):1061–1097.

Cope, V. 1988. "Third-party liability: victims' rights movement spurs expansion in law." *Trial* 24:85–87.

Copen, J. 1991. "Rape victims sue over safety: one plaintiff wins $17 million in a third-party suit against landlord." *ABA Journal* 77:34–35.

Institute for the Study of Sexual Assault. 1983. *Civil Sexual Assault Cases: Judgements and Settlements.* Vol. I. San Francisco: Institute for Sexual Assault. Also Volumes II and III, published in 1985 and 1987 respectively.

Keeley, P. J. 1990. "Who decides? Community safety conventions at the heart of tort liability." *Cleveland State Law Review* 30:315–90, Summer.

Kelner, J., and S. Robert. 1991. "Municipal liability for inadequate security." *New York Law Journal* 205:3.

Kennedy, D. B. 1993. "Architectural concerns regarding security and premises liability." *Journal of Architectural and Planning Research* 10(2):105–129.

Kuhlman, R. S. 1989. *Safe Places? Security Planning and Litigation.* Charlottesville, VA: Michie.

Lambert, T. F. Jr. 1983. "Educational institutions-liability for failure to protect female students from foreseeable sexual assault." *ATLA Law Reporter* 26:200–201.

———. 1984. "College liable for negligent failure to protect woman student from foreseeable sexual assault in campus parking lot." *ATLA Law Reporter* 27:442–44.

Law, J. K. 1988. "Answering the liability challenge." *Security Management* 32:71–74.

Loggans, S. E. 1985. "Rape as an intentional tort: first and third-party liability." *Trial* 20(10):45–48.

Milich, M. F. 1987. "Protecting commercial landlords from liability for criminal acts of third parties." *Real Estate Law Journal* 15:236–43.

Novac, S. and Associates. 1993. *Sexual Harassment of Tenants: Legal Remedies, Problems and Recommendations.* Toronto: Ontario Women's Directorate and Ministry of Housing.

Page, J. A. 1988. *The Law of Premises Liability* (2nd edition). Cincinnati: Anderson.

Reford, M. E. 1989. "Pennsylvania's college and university information act: the effect of campus security legislation on university liability for campus crime," *Dickinson Law Review* 94:179–97.

Reskin, L. R. 1986. "Common carriers must protect riders from assault." *ABA Journal* 72:90.

Sherman, L. 1989. "Violent stranger crime at a large hotel: a case study in risk assessment methods." *Security Journal* 1:40–46.

Sherman, L. W., and J. Klein. 1984. *Major Lawsuits Over Crime and Security: Trends and Patterns 1958–1982.* College Park, M.D.: Institute of Criminal Justice and Criminology, University of Maryland.

Silas, F. A. 1984. "Tenant safety: landlords losing in court." *ABA Journal* 70:38.

Spain, N. 1991. *The Law of Inadequate Security.* Boston: Butterworth.

Svalina N. B. 1985. "Pleading a duty to protect persons from criminal attack in Illinois." *Illinois Bar Journal*, August, 666–69.

Territo, L. 1983. "Campus rape: determining liability." *Trial* 19(9):100–103.

INDEX

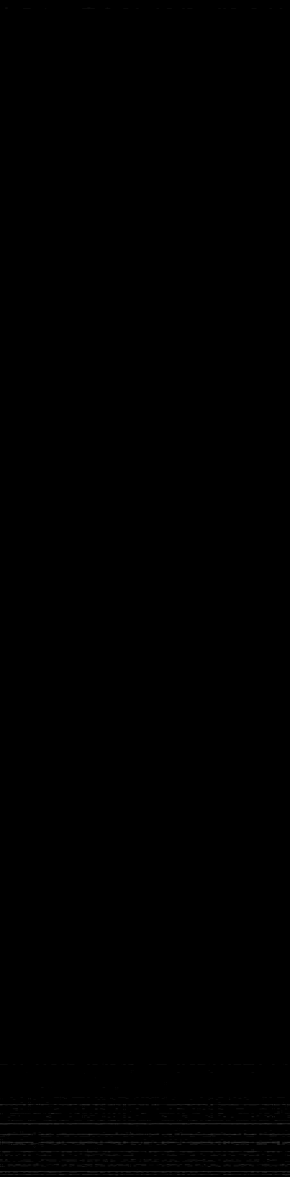

INDEX